# C# Markup for .NET MAUI Essentials

C# Markup for .NET MAUI Essentials

ISBN-13: 978-1-965764-41-1



Rev: 1.0

https://www.payloadbooks.com

# Contents

# Table of Contents

# 1. Start Here

This book provides a comprehensive guide to building cross-platform applications using .NET MAUI and C# Markup. Rather than relying on XAML, this approach focuses on constructing user interfaces entirely in C#, offering greater flexibility, consistency, and control over application structure and behavior. By combining modern development practices with a code-first approach, you will learn how to create applications that run across Android, iOS, macOS, and Windows from a single codebase.

The early chapters introduce the core concepts of .NET MAUI and C# Markup, including project structure, application lifecycle, and the fundamental building blocks of user interfaces. You will learn how views, layouts, and controls are combined to form responsive interfaces, and how to apply styling, theming, and reusable components to maintain consistency across your applications. Throughout these chapters, the emphasis is on understanding not only how to implement features, but also why they work the way they do.

As the book progresses, more advanced topics are introduced, including data binding, navigation, and application architecture. You will explore how to structure applications using patterns such as MVVM, manage state effectively, and connect user interfaces to underlying data models. Additional chapters cover platform features such as gestures, animations, and device capabilities, allowing you to create rich, interactive user experiences.

By the end of this book, you will have developed a solid understanding of how to design, build, and deploy cross-platform applications using .NET MAUI and C# Markup. Whether you are new to .NET MAUI or transitioning from XAML-based development, the knowledge and techniques presented in this book will provide a strong foundation for creating modern, maintainable applications.

## 1.1 Source Code Download

The source code and Visual Studio project files for the examples contained in this book are available for download at:

*https://www.payloadbooks.com/product/markupcode/*

## 1.2 Download the Color eBook

Thank you for purchasing the print edition of this book. Your purchase includes a color copy of the book in PDF format.

If you would like to download the PDF version of this book, please email proof of purchase (for example, a receipt, delivery notice, or photo of the physical book) to *info@payloadbooks.com*, and we will provide you with a download link.

## 1.3 Feedback

We want you to be satisfied with your purchase of this book. Therefore, if you find any errors in the book or have any comments, questions, or concerns, please contact us at *info@payloadbooks. com.*

## 1.4 Errata

While we make every effort to ensure the accuracy of the content of this book, inevitably, a book covering a subject area of this size and complexity may include some errors and oversights. Any known issues with the book will be outlined, together with solutions, at the following URL:

*https://www.payloadbooks.com/markuperrata/*

In the event that you find an error not listed in the errata, please let us know by emailing our technical support team at *info@payloadbooks.com.*

# 2. Introducing .NET MAUI and Declarative UI Design

The development of application user interfaces has changed significantly in recent years. In the past, developers wrote code that directly accessed UI toolkits, combined with static, XML-based layout designs, to create screens. Today, modern frameworks encourage developers to focus on state and declarative composition. Modern solutions like SwiftUI and Jetpack Compose introduced a new approach to building user interfaces by allowing developers to describe how the UI should look, rather than detailing each step of its construction. In the .NET ecosystem, the equivalent is provided by .NET Multi-platform App UI (MAUI) and specifically by the C# Markup approach to UI design.

## 2.1 The Evolution Toward Declarative UI

For decades, user interface design involved writing code to construct layout hierarchies manually, combined with UI design files typically created and modified using a user interface builder tool. Developers working with technologies like Windows Forms, WPF, or Xamarin.Forms often described layouts in XML-based markup, such as XAML, or built them dynamically using code-behind logic. While powerful, this style of UI construction could quickly become unwieldy, with repetitive boilerplate code, complex data bindings, and unclear separation between presentation and logic.

The emergence of declarative UI frameworks fundamentally changed this approach. Frameworks like React, SwiftUI, and Jetpack Compose all share a similar approach to app development. Instead of providing instructions on how to build and update the interface, we use a simple syntax to declare how the user interface should appear and behave. The framework is then responsible for ensuring that the rendered UI matches this state. This approach not only simplifies the logic behind the UI but also encourages cleaner and more maintainable code.

.NET developers can now benefit from this same declarative paradigm through .NET MAUI's C# Markup extensions. This approach enables developers to define UIs entirely in C# using a fluent, expressive, and type-safe syntax—without the need for XAML files.

## 2.2 Understanding .NET MAUI

.NET MAUI (Multi-platform App UI) is the evolution of Xamarin.Forms, designed to allow developers to build cross-platform applications that run natively on Android, iOS, macOS, and Windows from a single shared codebase. Unlike hybrid frameworks that rely on web technologies or embedded browsers, .NET MAUI compiles to native code and uses native UI controls on each platform. This means that applications built with .NET MAUI look, feel, and perform like true native apps, while developers only need to maintain one codebase.

Introducing .NET MAUI and Declarative UI Design

At its core, a .NET MAUI app defines its user interface using pages, layouts, and controls. Traditionally, these were defined using XAML—an XML-based markup language that describes UI hierarchies. XAML is powerful, but it requires developers to maintain two separate files per page: one for the markup and another for the C# logic behind it. This separation can lead to duplication and reduced readability, especially in small or dynamic projects.

C# Markup provides an alternative. Instead of splitting the UI across two languages, it allows developers to define the layout directly in C#, using an expressive and composable syntax. The result is a fully declarative UI built with the same language used for business logic, state management, and event handling.

## 2.3 What Is C# Markup?

C# Markup refers to a set of fluent APIs that make it possible to define user interfaces in a declarative style directly within C# code. It is part of the .NET MAUI Community Toolkit, an official extension library supported by Microsoft that enhances productivity and simplifies everyday tasks in .NET MAUI development.

Below is a simple example of a user interface written using C# Markup:

```csharp
using CommunityToolkit.Maui.Markup;


public class MainPage : ContentPage
{
    public MainPage()
    {
        Content = new VerticalStackLayout
        {
            Spacing = 25,
            Padding = 30,
            Children =
            {
                new Label()
                    .Text("Welcome to .NET MAUI with C# Markup!")
                    .Font(size: 24)
                    .CenterHorizontal(),

                new Button()
                    .Text("Click Me")
                    .Invoke(b => b.Clicked += OnButtonClicked)
                    .CenterHorizontal()
            }
        };
    }
```

```
void OnButtonClicked(object sender, EventArgs e)
{
    ((Button)sender).Text = "Button Clicked!";
}
```

## 2.4 Comparing C# Markup with Other Declarative Frameworks

If you have previously worked with SwiftUI or Jetpack Compose, you will recognize some similarities. Each of these frameworks defines UIs as hierarchies of elements that react to changes in data or state.

For example, the SwiftUI equivalent of the previous C# Markup example might read as follows:

```
VStack(spacing: 25) {
    Text("Welcome to SwiftUI!")
        .font(.system(size: 24))
    Button("Click Me") {
        print("Button clicked!")
    }
}
.padding(30)
```

The equivalent Jetpack Compose declaration is as follows:

```
Column(
    modifier = Modifier.padding(30.dp),
    verticalArrangement = Arrangement.spacedBy(25.dp)
) {
    Text("Welcome to Jetpack Compose!", fontSize = 24.sp)
    Button(onClick = { /* Handle click */ }) {
        Text("Click Me")
    }
}
```

While the syntax differs, the structure and logic are nearly identical. Each framework emphasizes readability, and state-driven design. In all cases, the UI is expressed as a tree of views, where each view's appearance and behavior are derived from data and application state.

## 2.5 Benefits of Using C# Markup

Adopting C# Markup in .NET MAUI projects provides several key advantages:

- **Unified Codebase** – All UI definitions, event handling, and business logic are written in one language (C#), reducing cognitive overhead and simplifying refactoring.

- **Type Safety and IntelliSense** – Because C# Markup uses the C# compiler directly, developers benefit from compile-time checking and full IntelliSense support in Integrated Development Environments (IDEs) such as Visual Studio.

- **Declarative and Readable** – The fluent syntax reads naturally and describes intent clearly, leading to cleaner and more maintainable code.

- **No XAML Parsing Overhead** – Eliminating XAML parsing (in other words, the processing work required to translate a XAML layout to the actual UI) can improve performance and reduce application size.

- **Composability and Reuse** – UI components can easily be factored into reusable C# classes, functions, or extension methods.

## 2.6 Looking Ahead

This book explores C# Markup in depth—from the basics of layout construction to advanced techniques for styling, data binding, and component reuse. You will learn how to build cross-platform applications entirely in C# using declarative principles similar to those found in SwiftUI and Jetpack Compose.

In the next chapter, we will walk through setting up your development environment, installing the required tools, and creating your first .NET MAUI project. From there, you will begin constructing your first C# Markup interface and see how declarative UI design can transform your development workflow.

# 3. Installing the .NET MAUI Development Environment

The first step in learning C# Markup and .NET MAUI is installing the development frameworks and tools. This chapter covers installing Visual Studio with the .NET MAUI workload, and the C# Markup packages.

By the end of this chapter, you will have a fully functional environment that allows you to build and run .NET MAUI projects using C# Markup.

## 3.1 Setting Up Visual Studio

While .NET MAUI projects can be developed with several Integrated Development Environments (IDEs), Visual Studio offers the richest experience, including project templates, device emulators, and integrated debugging.

Visual Studio is available in Community, Professional, and Enterprise editions. Though this book is based on the free Community edition of Visual Studio, you can also use the Professional or Enterprise editions if you already have or choose to purchase a paid license.

To complete the examples in this book, you will need Visual Studio 2026 or later (this book is based on Visual Studio 2026). Go to the following page to download the Visual Studio Installer:

*https://visualstudio.microsoft.com/downloads/*

Launch the installer and proceed through the initial screens until you reach the Workloads screen:

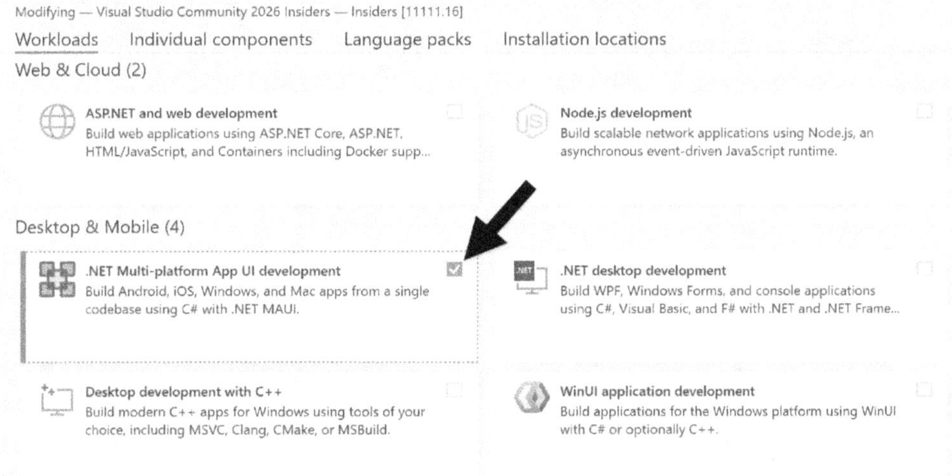


Figure 3-1

Installing the .NET MAUI Development Environment

In the Desktop & Mobile section of this screen, enable the ".NET Multiplatform App UI Development" option highlighted in Figure 3-1 before clicking the Install button.

Once the installation tasks have completed, launch Visual Studio if it does not start automatically:

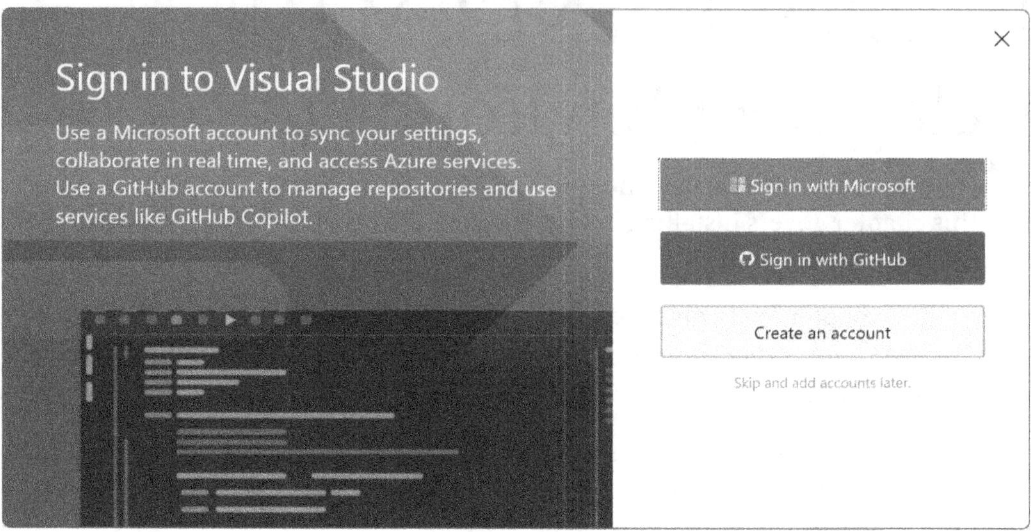


Figure 3-2

Sign in with your Microsoft account when prompted, then enable GitHub Copilot in the subsequent screen. Copilot is an AI assistant that uses ChatGPT to answer questions, resolve problems, and generate code for you. To complete the activation, you will need to create a GitHub account if you do not already have one.

Once Copilot has been activated, the project selection screen shown in Figure 3-3 will appear:

Figure 3-3

## 3.2 Creating a Visual Studio Project

Before we can begin working with C# Markup, we must install the MVVM Toolkit and C# Markup packages. The easiest way to install these packages, however, is from within a Visual Studio project. Now is also a good opportunity to check that Visual Studio and the .NET MAUI workload are installed and configured correctly. To create a new project, launch Visual Studio and select the "Create a new project" option to display the template selection dialog.

Use the search bar (marked A in Figure 3-4) or scroll through the templates to locate the .NET MAUI App option (B) and select it before clicking Next:

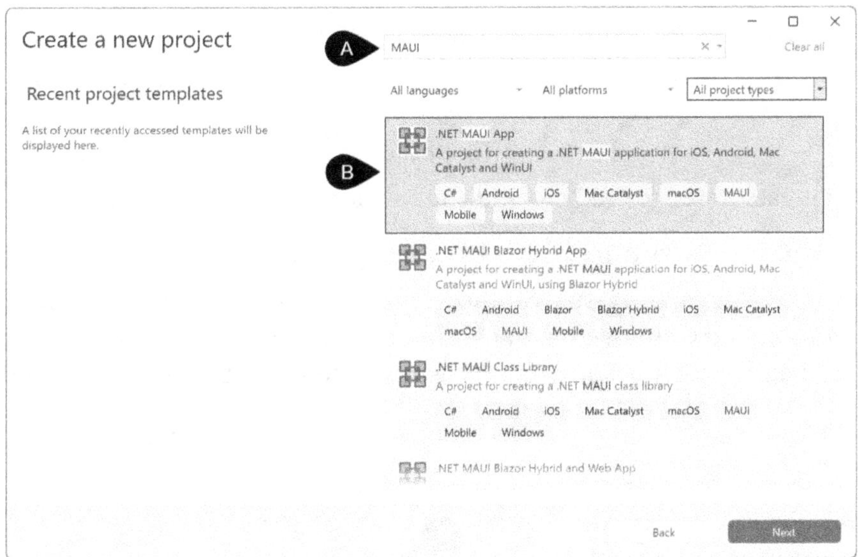

Figure 3-4

On the project configuration screen, name the project MauiDemo:

Figure 3-5

## Installing the .NET MAUI Development Environment

Click Next and, on the Additional information screen, select the .NET 10.0 (Long Term Support) framework, then click Create:

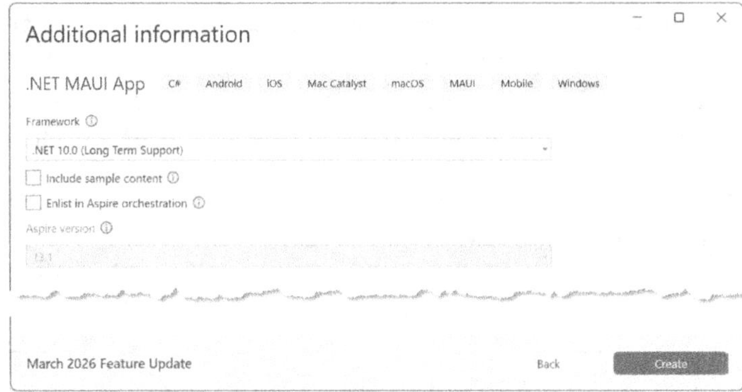

Figure 3-6

With the project created, we are ready to add support for C# Markup development.

## 3.3 Installing the MVVM and MAUI Markup packages

The right-hand side of the main Visual Studio window contains a tabbed panel. When a project is first created, the GitHub Copilot Chat panel (marked A in Figure 3-7) is typically displayed. To install the MVVM and Maui Markup Toolkits, we need to select the Solution Explorer tab (B).

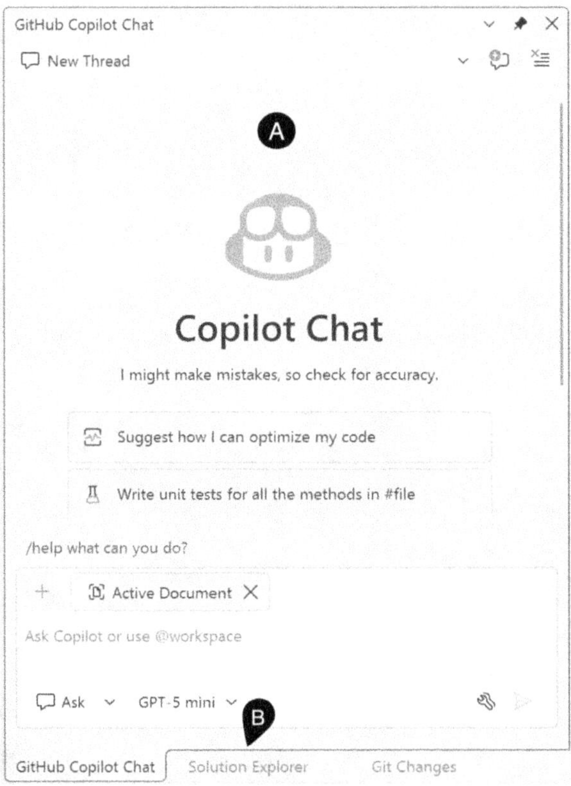



Figure 3-7

Within the Solution Explorer, right-click on the MauiDemo entry as highlighted in Figure 3-8 below, and select the *Manage NuGet Packages...* menu option:

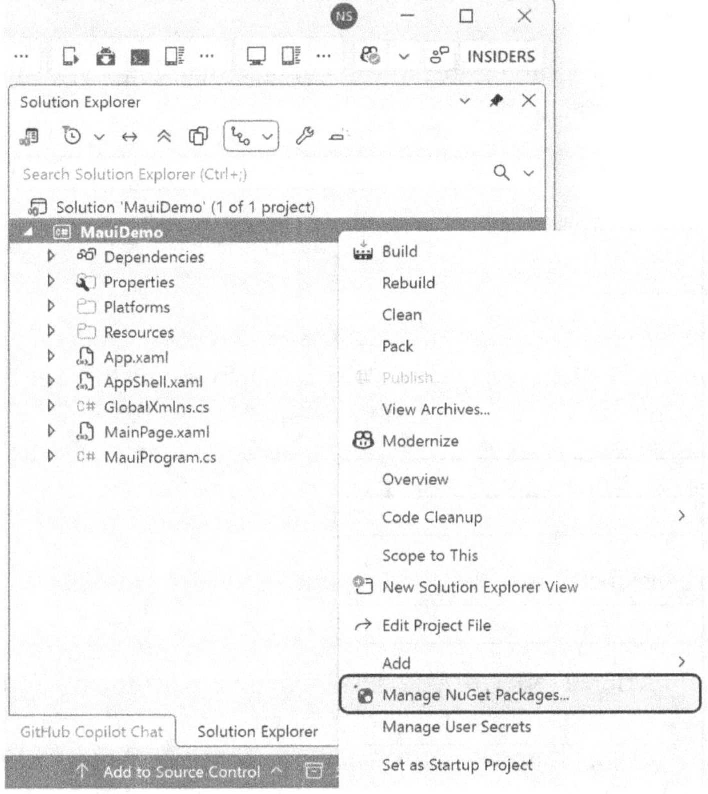

Figure 3-8

When the NuGet panel appears, select the Browse tab and enter "MVVM" into the search field. Select the CommunityToolkit.Mvvm option from the list of matching results, followed by the Install button:

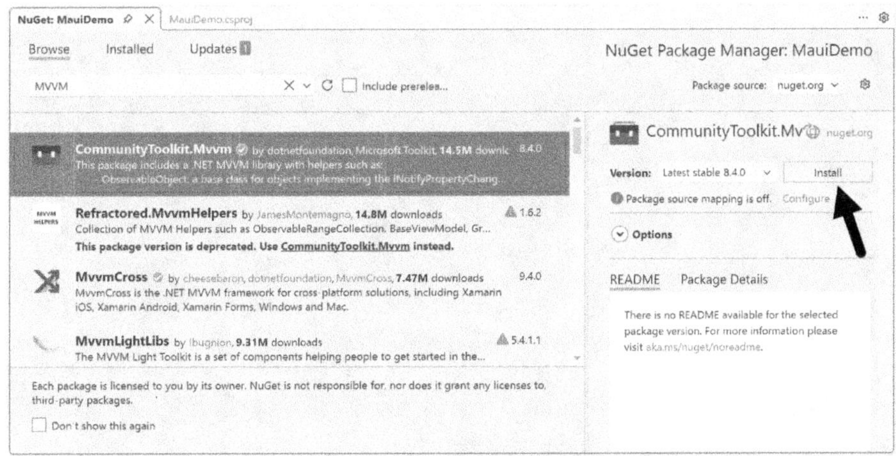

Figure 3-9

Installing the .NET MAUI Development Environment

Confirm the changes when prompted and agree to the license terms to complete the installation.

Remaining in the NuGet panel, search for and install the CommunityToolkit.Maui.Markup package using the above steps.

The C# Markup packages can be susceptible to version incompatibilities, leading to errors like the following during package installation:

```
Warning As Error: Detected package downgrade: Microsoft.Maui.Controls
from 10.0.41 to 10.0.20. Reference the package directly from the project
to select a different version.
 MauiDemo -> CommunityToolkit.Maui.Markup 7.0.1 -> Microsoft.Maui.
Controls (>= 10.0.41)
 MauiDemo -> Microsoft.Maui.Controls (>= 10.0.20)
```

In the above example, the NuGet package manager is informing us that the CommunityToolkit. Maui.Markup package requires a newer version of the Microsoft.Maui.Controls package than the one currently installed. To resolve this type of problem, search for the offending package in the NuGet manager and upgrade it to the latest version before retrying the original package installation.

Once the packages are installed, close the NuGet panel.

## 3.4 Summary

You now have a fully functional .NET MAUI development environment. You've installed Visual Studio, added .NET MAUI workloads and toolkits, configured your IDE, and confirmed everything is working correctly. With this foundation in place, you're ready to start writing declarative C# Markup code in the next chapter, where we'll explore how to construct your first user interface using C# syntax rather than XAML.

# 4. Building a C# Markup MAUI App

With Visual Studio installed and configured, the next step is to create an example .NET MAUI application using C# Markup. This chapter will demonstrate how to build a simple app entirely in C#, explaining each stage of the process and illustrating how declarative C# Markup replaces traditional XAML with a cleaner, more integrated approach.

## 4.1 Understanding the C# Markup Approach

C# Markup is a concise, declarative alternative to building user interfaces in XAML. Instead of maintaining separate XAML and C# code files, C# Markup lets us construct entire user interfaces directly in C#, combining layout definitions, styling, and logic in a single file. Because the UI is expressed in code, we gain access to the full power of the C# language, including variables, conditionals, and loops. It also provides a more unified development experience, as there is no longer a need to switch between XAML and code files.

## 4.2 Opening the MauiDemo Project

Begin by launching Visual Studio and opening the MauiDemo project created in the previous chapter. This project provides us with a basic cross-platform app structure ready to modify.

## 4.3 Changing the App Initialization Code

When a completed app runs, it executes code that initializes the underlying .NET MAUI toolkits. The default initialization code generated by Visual Studio for XAML-based development needs to be modified to initialize the markup-specific toolkit. To review the current code, display the Solution Explorer panel by selecting the tab marked A in Figure 4-1, then double-click on the *MauiProgram.cs* file (B) to open it in the code editor:

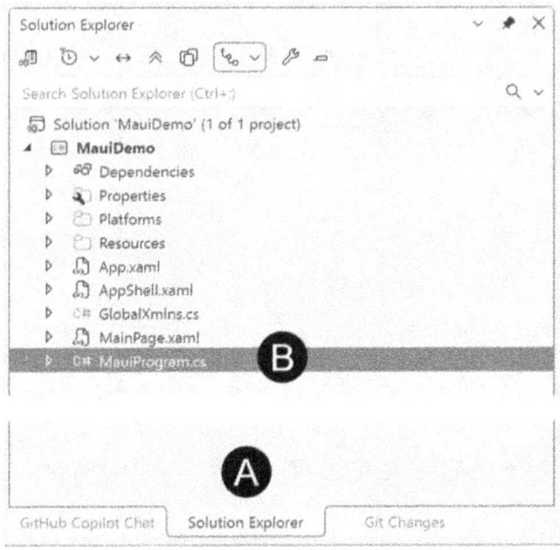


Figure 4-1

## Building a C# Markup MAUI App

The initialization code in the *MauiProgram.cs* file currently reads as follows:

```csharp
using Microsoft.Extensions.Logging;

namespace MauiDemo
{
    public static class MauiProgram
    {
        public static MauiApp CreateMauiApp()
        {
            var builder = MauiApp.CreateBuilder();
            builder
                .UseMauiApp<App>()
                .ConfigureFonts(fonts =>
                {
                    fonts.AddFont("OpenSans-Regular.ttf",
                                        "OpenSansRegular");
                    fonts.AddFont("OpenSans-Semibold.ttf",
                                        "OpenSansSemibold");
                });
#if DEBUG
            builder.Logging.AddDebug();
#endif
            return builder.Build();
        }
    }
}
```

To add support for C# Markup, we need to call the *UseMauiCommunityToolkitMarkup()* method on the MauiApp instance, as shown below:

```csharp
using Microsoft.Extensions.Logging;
using CommunityToolkit.Maui.Markup;

namespace MauiDemo
{
    public static class MauiProgram
    {
        public static MauiApp CreateMauiApp()
        {
            var builder = MauiApp.CreateBuilder();
            builder
                .UseMauiApp<App>()
                .UseMauiCommunityToolkitMarkup()
```

```
        .ConfigureFonts(fonts =>
        {
            fonts.AddFont("OpenSans-Regular.ttf",
                                "OpenSansRegular");
            fonts.AddFont("OpenSans-Semibold.ttf",
                                "OpenSansSemibold");
        });
#if DEBUG
        builder.Logging.AddDebug();
#endif
        return builder.Build();
    }
  }
}
```

This configuration step ensures that the C# Markup toolkit extensions are available throughout your project.

## 4.4 Removing the Old UI Design

When the project was created, Visual Studio generated several XAML files. The *MainPage.xaml* file is of particular significance because it contains the XAML-based UI design for the sample app. Since we will be redesigning the UI using C# Markup, the XAML file is redundant and can be deleted.

When Visual Studio generated the *MainPage.xaml* file, it also generated a C# class file called *MainPage.xaml.cs* containing the code to initialize and display the XAML UI layout and handle events (otherwise known as the "code-behind" file). The first step is to rename this file, otherwise it too will be deleted when we remove *MainPage.xaml*. Using the Solution Explorer, click on the disclosure arrow located to the left of the *MainPage.xaml* file to reveal the *MainPage.xaml.cs* file as indicated in Figure 4-2 below:

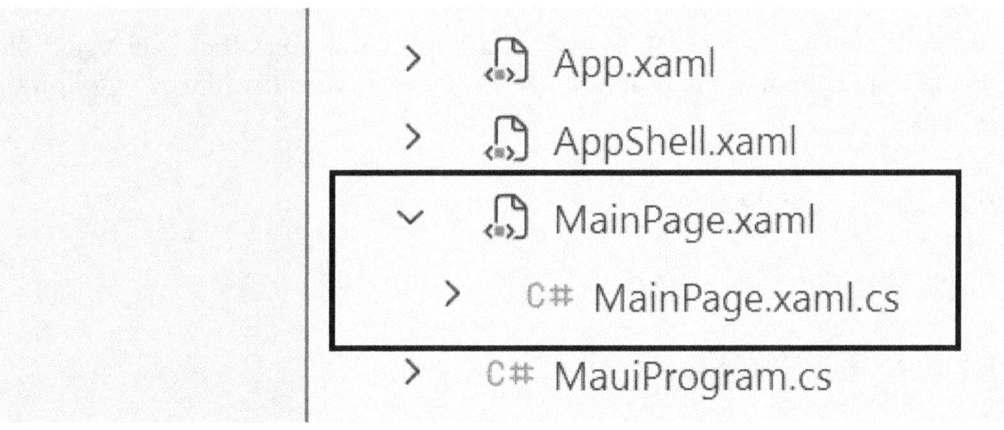


Figure 4-2

Building a C# Markup MAUI App

Right-click on the *MainPage.xaml.cs* file, select the "Open in File Explorer" menu option, and rename the file *MainPage.cs*.

Once the code-behind file has been renamed, return to the Solution Explorer, select the *MainPage.xaml* file, and press Delete on your keyboard to remove it from the project.

## 4.5 The AppShell.xaml file

Visual Studio also generated a file named *AppShell.xaml*. This file serves as a navigation and layout container, providing structure for apps with multiple pages, including page navigation and elements such as menus, tab bars, and navigation routes. The default *AppShell.xaml* file will resemble the following:

```
<?xml version="1.0" encoding="UTF-8" ?>
<Shell
    x:Class="MauiDemo.AppShell"
    xmlns="http://schemas.microsoft.com/dotnet/2021/maui"
    xmlns:x="http://schemas.microsoft.com/winfx/2009/xaml"
    xmlns:local="clr-namespace:MauiDemo"
    Title="MauiDemo">

    <ShellContent
        Title="Home"
        ContentTemplate="{DataTemplate local:MainPage}"
        Route="MainPage" />
</Shell>
```

The above example declares a top-level Shell view containing a single ShellContent element configured to display the MainPage UI with the title text set to "Home". Later in the book, we explain how to migrate this structure to C# Markup and implement navigation. For this example, however, we will leave the file unchanged.

## 4.6 Building the Main Page with C# Markup

The next step is to design the new UI using C# Markup. Double-click the *MainPage.cs* file in the Solution Explorer to open it in the code editor. Once opened, the file will read as follows:

```
namespace MauiDemo
{
    public partial class MainPage : ContentPage
    {
        int count = 0;

        public MainPage()
        {
            InitializeComponent();
        }
```

```csharp
    private void OnCounterClicked(object? sender, EventArgs e)
    {
        count++;

        if (count == 1)
            CounterBtn.Text = $"Clicked {count} time";
        else
            CounterBtn.Text = $"Clicked {count} times";

        SemanticScreenReader.Announce(CounterBtn.Text);
    }
}
```

In the code above, the MainPage() method calls InitializeComponent(), which initializes and displays the layout defined in the XAML file. Having discarded the XAML layout, we will delete this call and replace it with the C# Markup for our new UI. Edit the file and make the following changes:

```csharp
using CommunityToolkit.Maui.Markup;

namespace MauiDemo
{
    public partial class MainPage : ContentPage
    {
        int count = 0;

        public MainPage()
        {
            InitializeComponent();

            Content = new VerticalStackLayout
            {
                Spacing = 20,
                Padding = new Thickness(30),
                Children =
                {
                    new Label()
                        .Text("Welcome to .NET MAUI and C# Markup")
                        .Font(size: 24)
                        .CenterHorizontal(),
```

```csharp
                    new Button()
                        .Text("Click Me")
                        .CenterHorizontal()
                        .Invoke(b => b.Clicked += OnButtonClicked)
            }
        };
    }


    void OnButtonClicked(object? sender, EventArgs e)
    {
        count++;

        if (sender is Button button)
        {
            if (count == 1)
                button.Text = $"Clicked {count} time";
            else
                button.Text = $"Clicked {count} times";
        }
    }
    private void OnCounterClicked(object? sender, EventArgs e)
    {
        count++;

        if (count == 1)
            CounterBtn.Text = $"Clicked {count} time";
        else
            CounterBtn.Text = $"Clicked {count} times";

        SemanticScreenReader.Announce(CounterBtn.Text);
    }
    }
}
```

The modified code defines a VerticalStackLayout as the page's *root container*, with spacing and padding applied to maintain layout consistency. Within this container, a Label displays a welcome message, and a Button allows the user to interact with the interface. When the button is clicked, the OnButtonClicked event handler increments the counter variable and updates the Button view's text accordingly. All of this is achieved through fluent C# syntax rather than separate XAML markup.

## 4.7 Running the App

Until we set up Visual Studio to run apps on iOS and Android emulators and devices, we will run MauiDemo as a Windows app. In the Visual Studio toolbar, make sure that the run button is set to "Windows Machine" before clicking it to launch the app:

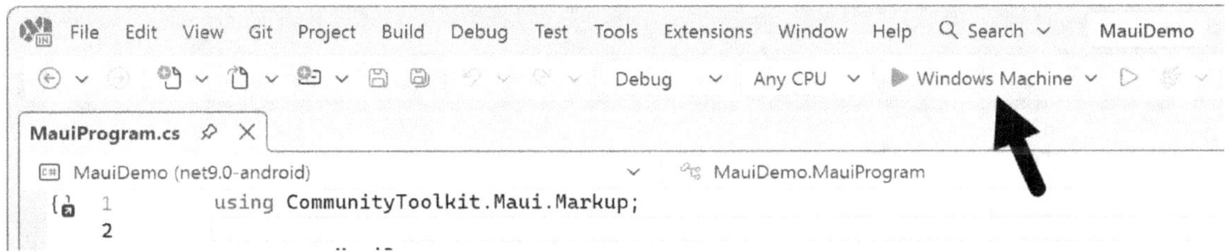

Figure 4-3

When the app launches, you should see the welcome message and the clickable button as illustrated in Figure 4-4. Interacting with the button triggers the event handler, which updates the button text in real time:

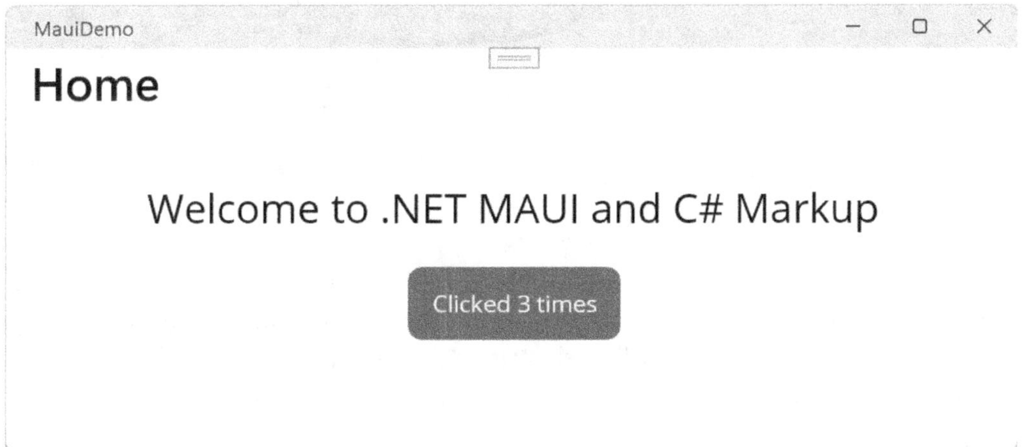


Figure 4-4

Note that the "Home" page title appears as declared in the *AppShell.xaml* file and can be removed if not required:

## 4.8 Exporting the Project Template

At this point, we have created a Visual Studio .NET MAUI project named MauiDemo and installed the MVVM Toolkit and C# Markup packages. We have also migrated the project UI from XAML to C# Markup.

Although we have performed these tasks, they only apply to the current project (in this case, MauiDemo). To avoid manually repeating these steps for each new project, a better approach is to export the modified MauiDemo template and use it as the basis for future projects.

To keep our MauiDemo solution intact, we will begin by making a copy of the solution folder to use for the template. Referring to the Solution Explorer, right-click on the top entry (Solution

# Building a C# Markup MAUI App

'MauiDemo' (1 of 1 project)) and select the "Open in File Explorer" menu option as demonstrated in Figure 4-5:

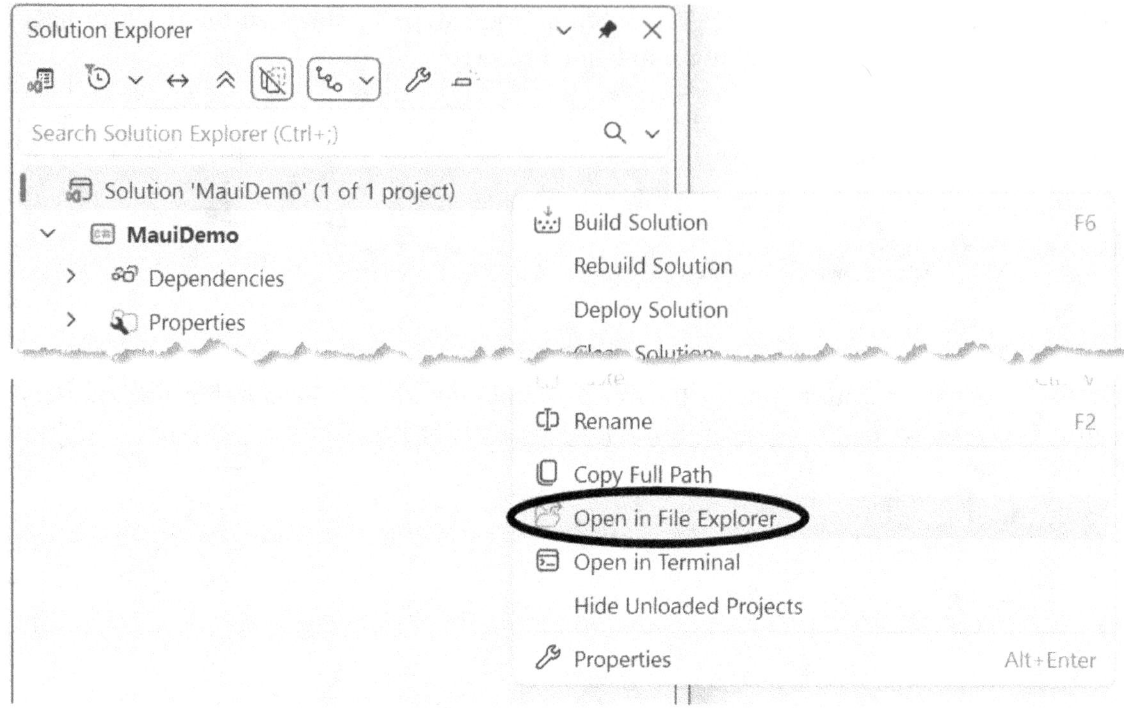

Figure 4-5

Select the *File -> Close Solution* menu option, then, within File Explorer, navigate up one level to the parent folder and then copy and paste the entire MauiDemo folder, naming the copy *MauiTemplate*. Return to Visual Studio, select the "Open a project or solution" option, then navigate to the MauiTemplate solution folder and open the *MauiDemo.slnx* file.

Next, edit the *MainPage.cs* file and remove the example code so that we don't have to delete it each time we use the template:

```
using CommunityToolkit.Maui.Markup;

namespace MauiDemo
{
    public partial class MainPage : ContentPage
    {
        int count = 0;

        public MainPage()
        {
            Content = new VerticalStackLayout
            {
                Spacing = 20,
```

```csharp
            Padding = new Thickness(30),
            Children =
            {
                new Label()
                    .Text("Welcome to .NET MAUI and C# Markup")
                    .Font(size: 24)
                    .CenterHorizontal(),

                new Button()
                    .Text("Click Me")
                    .CenterHorizontal()
                    .Invoke(b => b.Clicked += OnButtonClicked)
            }
        };
    }

    void OnButtonClicked(object? sender, EventArgs e)
    {
        count++;

        if (sender is Button button)
        {
            if (count == 1)
                button.Text = $"Clicked {count} time";
            else
                button.Text = $"Clicked {count} times";
        }
    }
}
```

To export the template, select the *Project -> Export Template...* menu option, then choose the "Project template" option in the template wizard dialog. Click Next and enter the following information on the subsequent screen:

- **Name** - MAUIMarkup

- **Description** - A project for creating a .NET MAUI application using C# Markup

Finally, enable the "Automatically import the template into Visual Studio" and "Display an explorer window on the output files folder" options, then click the Finish button:

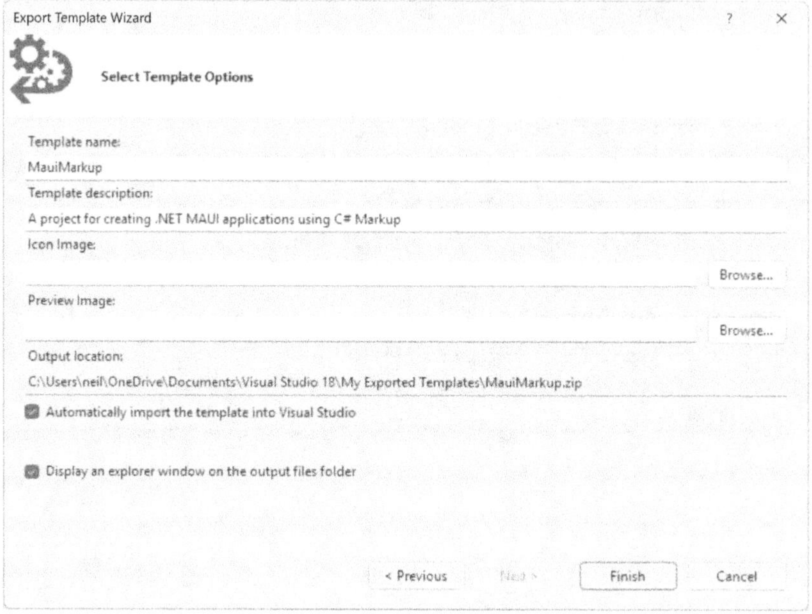

Figure 4-6

If Visual Studio reports that it was unable to save the template, refer to the explorer window, delete the parent "My Exported Templates" folder, and repeat the export steps.

Next time we create a new project in Visual Studio, the MAUIMarkup template will appear in the template selection screen as shown in Figure 4-7:

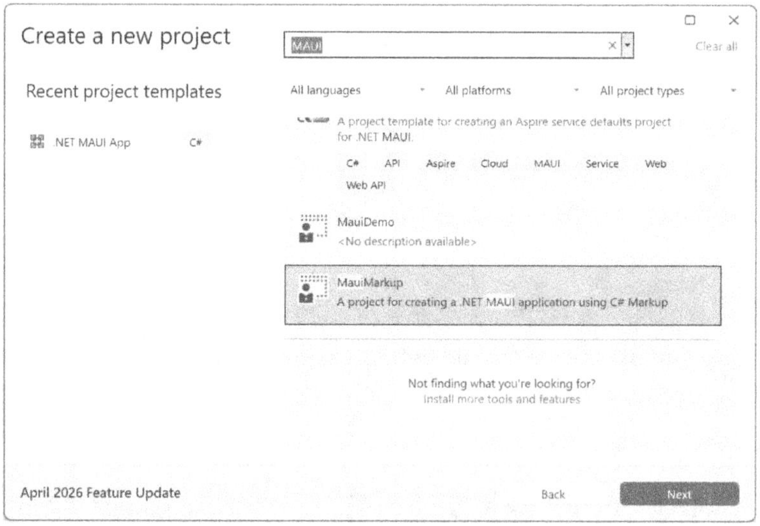

Figure 4-7

## 4.9 Understanding Fluent Syntax

One of the defining features of C# Markup is its fluent syntax. This design pattern allows properties and methods to be chained together in a readable, declarative manner. For example, the following code creates a label, sets its text and font size, and aligns it horizontally in a single statement:

```
new Label()
    .Text("Hello")
    .Font(size: 18)
    .CenterHorizontal();
```

Each chained call operates on the same object, making the interface's structure easy to read and maintain. This approach not only improves clarity but also provides IntelliSense support in the code editor, allowing you to discover properties and methods interactively as you type. For example, we can change the background color of our Button view as follows:

```
new Button()
    .Text("Click Me")
    .BackgroundColor(Colors.DarkSeaGreen)
    .CenterHorizontal()
    .Invoke(b => b.Clicked += OnButtonClicked)
```

## 4.10 Summary

In this chapter, we completed our first .NET MAUI application using C# Markup. We learned how to remove redundant XAML markup and migrate to C# Markup. We then constructed and tested a simple interface using declarative syntax, including event handling.

Finally, we exported the project template to save time when creating new .NET MAUI C# Markup projects.

# 5. Testing on the Android Emulator

During development, it is often necessary to build and test applications quickly without deploying to a physical device. The Android emulator provides a virtual device environment in which apps can be installed, run, and debugged directly from Visual Studio. By simulating different hardware configurations and device types, the emulator allows applications to be tested under a wide range of conditions. In this chapter, we will create and configure Android Virtual Devices (AVDs) and run applications on the emulator.

## 5.1 About Android Virtual Devices

Android Virtual Devices are emulators that allow Android applications to be tested without installing them on a physical Android device. An AVD may be configured to emulate various hardware features, including screen size, memory capacity, and the presence or absence of features such as a camera, GPS navigation, or an accelerometer. Several emulator templates are installed as part of the standard Visual Studio installation, allowing AVDs to be configured for various devices. Custom configurations can be created to match any physical Android device by specifying properties such as processor type, memory capacity, screen size, and pixel density.

New AVDs are created and managed using the Android Virtual Device Manager, which may be used in command-line mode or with a more user-friendly graphical user interface.

## 5.2 Creating an Android Virtual Device

The first step in setting up Android testing is creating an AVD. Begin by launching Visual Studio and selecting the *Tools -> Android -> Android Device Manager...* menu option to display the dialog shown in Figure 5-1:

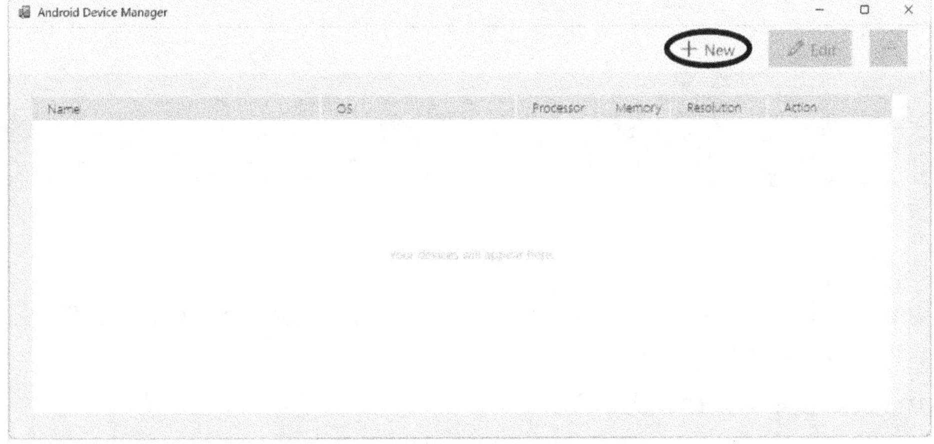

Figure 5-1

Click the + New button highlighted above to create a new virtual device. In the New Device dialog

Testing on the Android Emulator

shown in Figure 5-2, use the menus marked A to select a base device, processor architecture, and Android operating system version. Change the device name using the text field (B) if necessary. For this example, we will create a Pixel 9 device configured with Android 16.0 (API 36) with Google Play Store support:

Figure 5-2

The device manager will configure the device settings to match the base model, details of which can be reviewed and modified in the property table (C).

Once the device has been configured, click the Create button (D) to download and install the AVD image and, when prompted, review and accept the licensing terms and conditions. The main AVD manager window will list the new virtual device and display the download and installation progress:

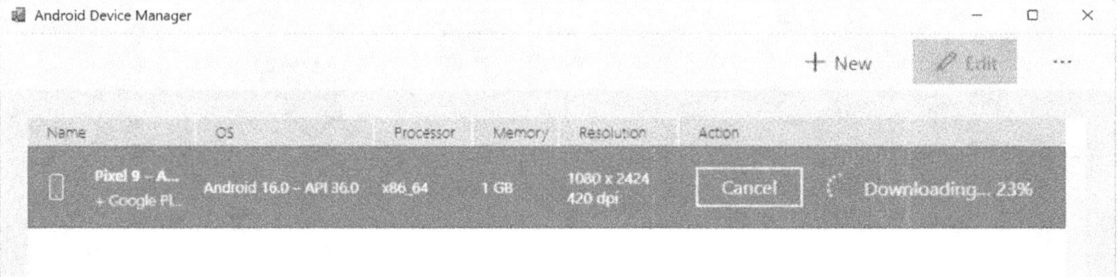

Figure 5-3

When the download is complete, the AVD is ready to use. Close the Android Device Manager dialog and return to the main Visual Studio window.

## 5.3 Running the app on the AVD

To test the current app on the virtual device, click the run target menu in the toolbar and select the new AVD from the Android Emulators sub-menu, as shown in Figure 5-4:

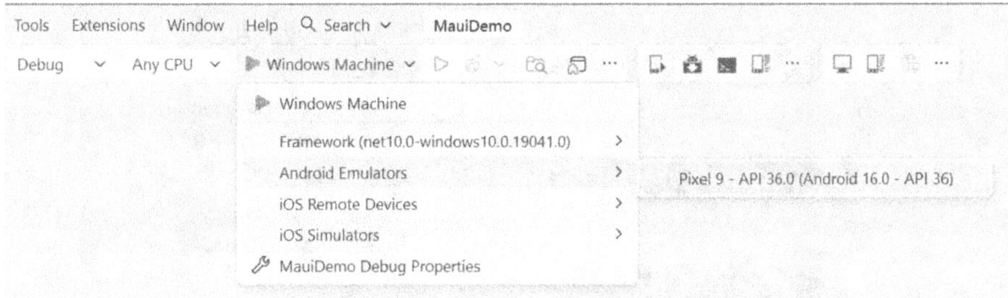

Figure 5-4

With the Android emulator selected, click the run button to start the AVD emulator, build the app, and run it on the virtual device. Keep in mind that it may take a few minutes for the Android emulator to boot before the app fully launches. The emulator displays an initial splash screen during loading. Once loaded, the main emulator window appears, containing a representation of the chosen device type (in the case of Figure 5-5, this is a Pixel 9 device):

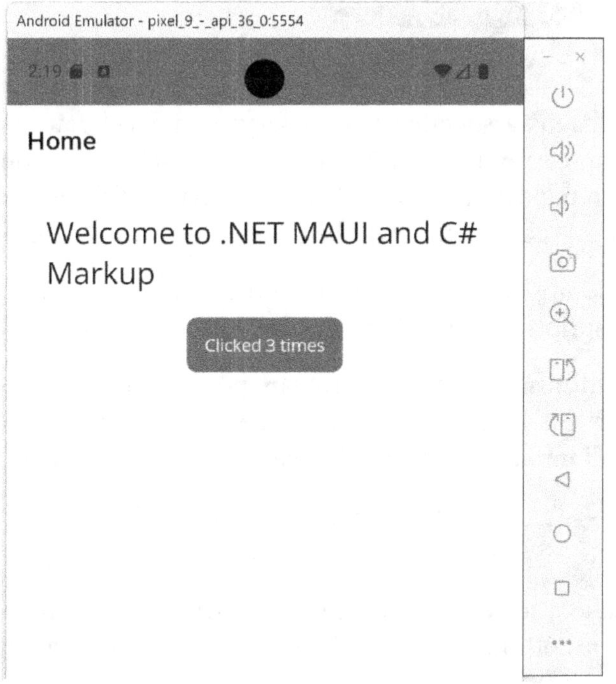


Figure 5-5

The toolbar positioned along the right-hand edge of the window provides quick access to the emulator controls and configuration options.

## 5.4 Emulator Toolbar Options

The emulator toolbar (Figure 5-6) provides access to a range of options relating to the appearance and behavior of the emulator environment.

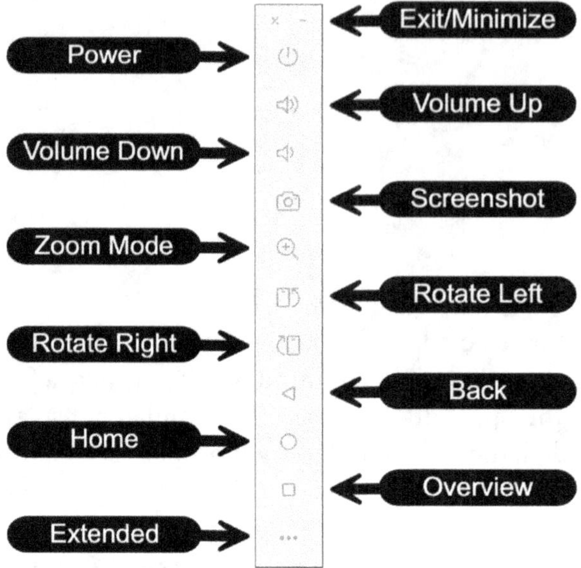


Figure 5-6

Each button in the toolbar is associated with a keyboard accelerator, which can be identified either by hovering the mouse pointer over the button and waiting for the tooltip to appear or via the help option of the extended controls panel. Though many of the options contained within the toolbar are self-explanatory, each option will be covered for the sake of completeness:

- **Exit / Minimize** – The uppermost 'x' button in the toolbar exits the emulator session when selected, while the '-' option minimizes the entire window.

- **Power** – The Power button simulates the hardware power button on a physical Android device. Clicking and releasing this button will lock the device and turn off the screen. Clicking and holding this button will initiate the device "Power off" request sequence.

- **Volume Up / Down** – Two buttons that control the audio volume of playback within the simulator environment.

- **Take Screenshot** – Takes a screenshot of the device's screen. The captured image is stored at the location specified in the Settings screen of the extended controls panel, as outlined later in this chapter.

- **Zoom Mode** – This button toggles in and out of zoom mode, details of which will be covered later in this chapter.

- **Rotate Left/Right** – Rotates the emulated device between portrait and landscape orientations.

- **Back** – Performs the standard Android "Back" navigation to return to a previous screen.

- **Home** – Displays the device's home screen.

- **Overview** – Simulates selection of the standard Android "Overview" navigation, which displays the currently running apps on the device.

- **Fold Device** – Simulates the folding and unfolding of a foldable device. This option is only available if the emulator is running a foldable device system image.

- **Extended Controls** – Displays the extended controls panel, allowing for the configuration of options such as simulated location and telephony activity, battery strength, cellular network type, and fingerprint identification.

## 5.5 Working in Zoom Mode

The zoom button on the emulator toolbar toggles between zoom modes. When zoom mode is active, the toolbar button is depressed, and the mouse pointer appears as a magnifying glass when hovering over the device screen. Clicking the left mouse button zooms in relative to the selected point on the screen, with repeated clicks increasing the zoom level. Conversely, clicking the right mouse button decreases the zoom level. Toggling the zoom button off reverts the display to the default size.

Clicking and dragging while in zoom mode defines a rectangular area into which the view zooms when the mouse button is released. While in Zoom mode, the screen's visible area may be panned using the horizontal and vertical scrollbars located within the emulator window.

## 5.6 Resizing the Emulator Window

The emulator window's size (and the device's corresponding representation) can be changed at any time by clicking and dragging on any of the corners or sides of the window.

## 5.7 Extended Control Options

The extended controls toolbar button displays the panel illustrated in Figure 5-7. By default, the display settings will be shown. Selecting a different category from the left-hand panel will display the corresponding group of controls:

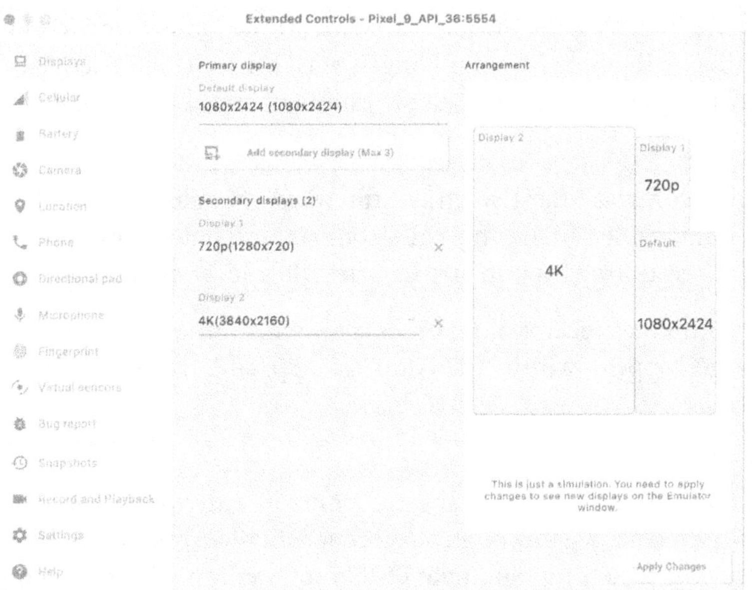

Figure 5-7

Testing on the Android Emulator

## 5.7.1 Displays

The display settings screen lets you add additional screen sizes to the emulator so apps can be tested on various device sizes. To add display sizes, click the "Add secondary display" button, then change the screen dimensions in the drop-down menu. Click the Apply Changes button to create the displays, which will appear beside the default display in the emulator window. The emulator supports three secondary screens in addition to the default display.

## 5.7.2 Cellular

The type of cellular connection being simulated can be changed within the cellular settings screen. Options are available to simulate different network types (CSM, EDGE, HSDPA, etc.) and a range of voice and data scenarios, including roaming and denied access.

## 5.7.3 Battery

Various battery states and charging conditions can be simulated on this panel of the extended controls screen, including battery charge level, battery health, and whether the AC charger is currently connected.

## 5.7.4 Camera

The emulator simulates a 3D scene when the camera is active. This takes the form of the interior of a virtual building, which you can navigate by holding down the Alt key while using the mouse and keyboard keys when recording video or before taking a photo within the emulator. This extended configuration option allows different images to be uploaded for display within the virtual environment.

## 5.7.5 Location

The location controls allow simulated location information to be sent to the emulator as decimal or sexagesimal coordinates. Location information can take the form of a single location or a sequence of points representing the device's movement, the latter provided in a file in either the GPS Exchange (GPX) or Keyhole Markup Language (KML) format. Alternatively, the integrated Google Maps panel may be used to select single points or travel routes visually.

## 5.7.6 Phone

The phone's extended controls offer two straightforward yet helpful simulations in the emulator. The first option simulates an incoming call from a designated phone number. This can be particularly useful when testing how an app handles high-level interrupts.

The second option simulates receipt of text messages within the emulator session. As in the real world, these messages appear within the Message app and trigger the standard notifications within the emulator.

## 5.7.7 Directional Pad

A directional pad (D-Pad) is an additional set of controls either built into an Android device or connected externally (such as a game controller) that provides directional controls (left, right, up, down). The directional pad settings simulate D-Pad interaction within the emulator.

### 5.7.8 Microphone

The microphone settings enable the microphone and simulate virtual headset and microphone connections. A button is also provided to launch the Voice Assistant on the emulator.

### 5.7.9 Fingerprint

Many Android devices now include built-in fingerprint detection hardware. The AVD emulator allows fingerprint authentication testing without running apps on a physical device with a fingerprint sensor. Details on configuring fingerprint testing within the emulator will be covered later in this chapter.

### 5.7.10 Virtual Sensors

The virtual sensors option simulates the accelerometer and magnetometer to emulate the effects of a device's physical motion, such as rotation, movement, and tilting, via yaw, pitch, and roll settings.

### 5.7.11 Bug report

Use this screen if you encounter a problem while using the emulator and want to submit a bug report to Google.

### 5.7.12 Snapshots

Snapshots capture the state of the currently running AVD session and can be saved and rapidly restored, making it easy to return the emulator to an exact state. Snapshots are covered later in this chapter.

### 5.7.13 Record and Playback

Allows the emulator screen and audio to be recorded and saved in WebM or animated GIF format.

### 5.7.14 Google Play

If the emulator is running a version of Android with Google Play Services installed, this option displays the current Google Play version. It also allows you to update the emulator to the latest version.

### 5.7.15 Settings

The settings panel provides a small group of configuration options. Use this panel to choose a darker theme for the toolbar and extended controls panel, specify a file system location where screenshots are saved, configure OpenGL support levels, and configure the emulator window to appear on top of other windows on the desktop.

### 5.7.16 Help

The Help screen contains three sub-panels: a list of keyboard shortcuts, links to access the emulator's online documentation, file bugs, and send feedback, and emulator version information.

## 5.8 Working with Snapshots

When an emulator starts for the first time, it performs a cold boot, much like a physical Android device when powered on. This cold boot process can take some time to complete as the operating system loads and background processes start. To avoid the need to go through this process every time the emulator starts, the system is configured to automatically save a snapshot (referred to as a *quick-boot snapshot*) of the emulator's current state when it exits. The next time the emulator is launched, the quick-boot snapshot is loaded into memory, and execution resumes from where it left off, allowing the emulator to restart in a fraction of the time required for a cold boot.

The Snapshots screen of the extended controls panel can store additional snapshots at any point during the execution of the emulator. This saves the entire emulator's state, allowing it to be restored to the exact point in time when the snapshot was taken. From within the screen, snapshots can be taken using the *Take Snapshot* button (marked A in Figure 5-8). To restore an existing snapshot, select it from the list (B) and click the run button (C) located at the bottom of the screen. Options are also provided to edit (D) the snapshot name and description and to delete (E) the currently selected snapshot:

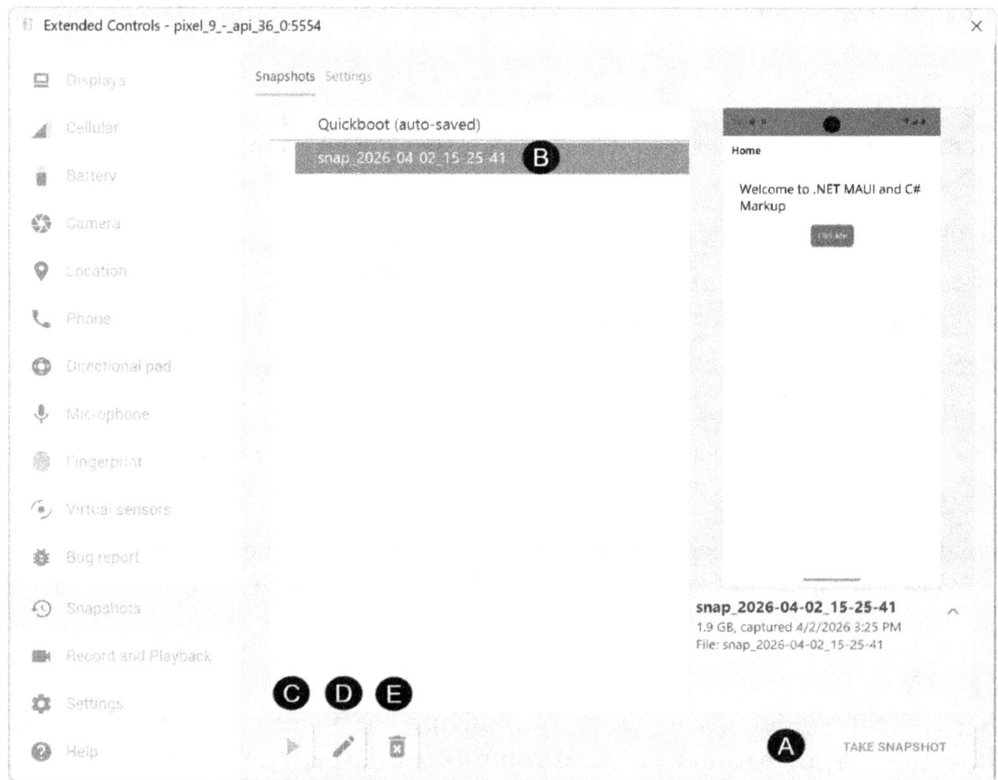


Figure 5-8

## 5.9 Configuring Fingerprint Emulation

The emulator allows up to 10 simulated fingerprints to be configured and used to test fingerprint authentication within Android apps. Configuring simulated fingerprints begins by launching the emulator, opening the Settings app, and selecting the Security option.

Within the Security settings screen, select the fingerprint option. On the resulting information screen, click on the *Next* button to proceed to the Fingerprint setup screen. Before fingerprint security can be enabled, a backup screen unlocking method (such as a PIN) must be configured.

Enter and confirm a suitable PIN and complete the PIN entry process by accepting the default notifications option.

Proceed through the remaining screens until the Settings app requests a fingerprint on the sensor. At this point, display the extended controls dialog, select the *Fingerprint* category in the left-hand panel, and make sure that *Finger 1* is selected in the main settings panel:

Figure 5-9

Click on the *Touch Sensor* button to simulate Finger 1 touching the fingerprint sensor. The emulator will report the successful addition of the fingerprint:

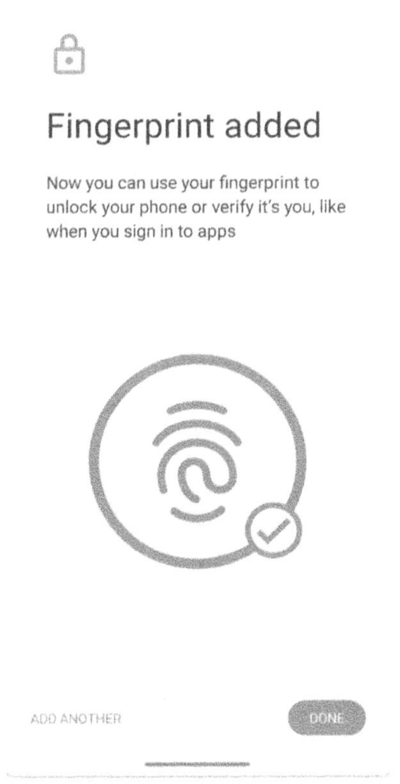


Figure 5-10

To add additional fingerprints, click on the *Add Another* button and select another finger from the extended controls panel menu before clicking on the *Touch Sensor* button again.

## 5.10 Summary

A typical application development process follows a cycle of coding, compiling, and running in a test environment. Android applications may be tested on a physical Android device or an Android Virtual Device (AVD) emulator. AVDs are created and managed using the Android Studio Device Manager tool, which may be used as a command-line tool or via a graphical user interface. When creating an AVD to simulate a specific Android device model, the virtual device should be configured with a hardware specification matching that of the physical device.

# 6. Testing .NET MAUI Apps on a Physical Android Device

While much can be achieved by testing applications on an Android Virtual Device (AVD), there is no substitute for real-world testing on a physical Android device, and some Android features are only available on physical devices.

Communication with both AVD instances and connected Android devices is handled by the *Android Debug Bridge (ADB).* This chapter explains how to configure the ADB environment to enable application testing on an Android device with Visual Studio.

## 6.1 An Overview of the Android Debug Bridge (ADB)

The primary purpose of the ADB is to facilitate interaction between a development system (in this case, Visual Studio) and both AVD emulators and Android devices for running and debugging applications.

The ADB consists of a client, a server process running in the background on the development system, and a daemon background process running in either AVDs or real Android devices such as phones and tablets.

The ADB client can take a variety of forms. For example, a client is provided as a command-line tool named *adb* in the Android SDK *platform-tools* sub-directory. Similarly, Visual Studio also has a built-in client.

## 6.2 Working with the ADB Command-line Client

The adb client tool is installed with Visual Studio and located in the Android SDK folder. Selecting the Visual Studio *Tools -> Android -> Android Adb Command Prompt...* menu option, or clicking the toolbar icon highlighted in Figure 6-1, will open a command-prompt window with the Android SDK platform-tools folder included in the system PATH environment variable:

Figure 6-1

Testing .NET MAUI Apps on a Physical Android Device

At the command prompt, enter adb to check that the executable is found:

```
C:\> adb
```

Alternatively, the SDK path can be added to the system PATH variable so that adb can be executed from any command prompt. Before adding it to the PATH environment variable, we must locate the Android SDK. To do so, select the Visual Studio *Tools -> Options* menu option and navigate to the *.NET MAUI -> Android* category in the left-hand panel (marked A in Figure 6-2):

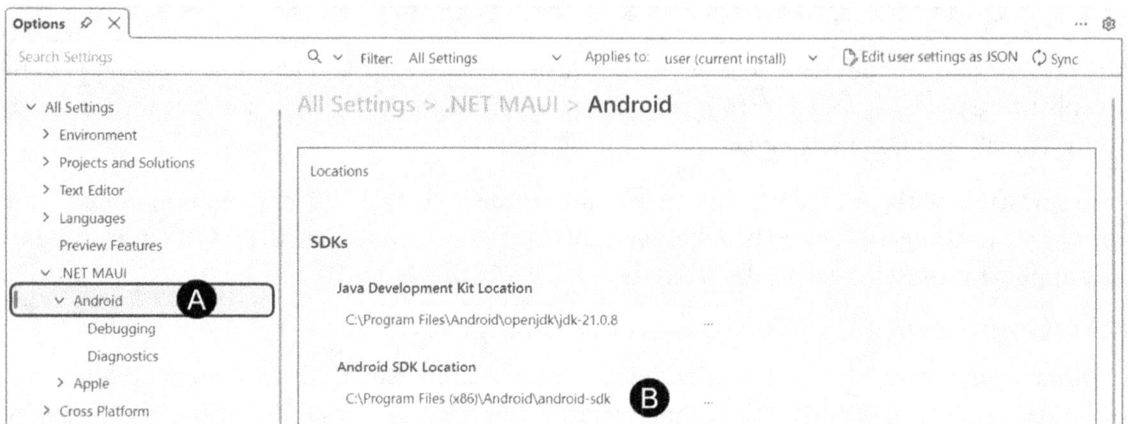



Figure 6-2

Next, copy the path assigned to the Android SDK Location field (B), then use the following steps to add the SDK tools to the system PATH environment variable:

1. Click the Start button located in the taskbar, enter *Edit the system environment variables* into the search bar and select the matching result. When the System Properties window appears, click the *Environment Variables...* button.

2. In the Environment Variables dialog, locate the Path variable in the System variables list, select it, and click the *Edit...* button. Using the *New* button in the edit dialog, add a new entry to the path. For example, assuming the Android SDK was installed into *C:\Program Files (x86)\Android\android-sdk*, the following entry would need to be added:

```
C:\Program Files (x86)\Android\android-sdk\platform-tools
```

3. Click OK in each dialog box, then close the System Properties control panel.

Open a command prompt window by pressing Windows + R, then entering cmd in the Run dialog. Within the Command Prompt window, enter:

```
C:\>  echo %Path%
C:\Windows\system32;C:\Windows;C:\Windows\System32\Wbem;C:\Windows\
System32\WindowsPowerShell\v1.0\;C:\Windows\System32\OpenSSH\;C:\Program
Files\dotnet\;C:\Program Files (x86)\Android\android-sdk\platform-
tools;C:\Users\neil\AppData\Local\Microsoft\WindowsApps;C:\Users\demo\.
dotnet\tools
```

The returned path variable value should include the paths to the Android SDK platform tools folders. Verify that the *platform-tools* value is correct by attempting to run the *adb* tool as follows:

```
C:\> adb
```

The tool should output a list of command-line options when executed.

If a message similar to the following appears for one or both of the commands, it is most likely that an incorrect path was appended to the Path environment variable:

```
'adb' is not recognized as an internal or external command,
operable program or batch file.
```

A variety of tasks may be performed using the *adb* command-line tool. For example, active virtual or physical devices may be listed using the *devices* command-line argument.

The following command output indicates the presence of an AVD on the system but no physical devices:

```
C:\> adb devices
List of devices attached
emulator-5554    device
```

The following output indicates that an Android device is connected to the system, but is not yet enabled for USB debugging:

```
C:\> adb devices
List of devices attached
R9WN80H2TWJ     unauthorized
```

## 6.3 Enabling USB Debugging ADB on Android Devices

Before ADB can connect to an Android device, the device must be configured to allow connections. On phone and tablet devices running Android 6.0 or later, the steps to achieve this are as follows:

1.  Open the Settings app on the device and select the *About tablet* or *About phone* option (on some versions of Android, this can be found on the *System* page of the Settings app).

2.  On the *About* screen, scroll down to the *Build number* field (Figure 6-3), then tap it 7 times until a message indicates that developer mode has been enabled. If the Build number is not listed on the About screen, it may be available via the *Software information* option. Alternatively, unfold the Advanced section of the list if available.

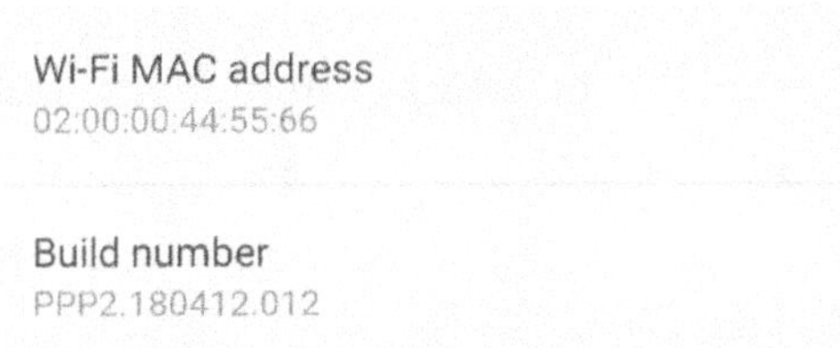


Figure 6-3

3.  Return to the main Settings screen and note the appearance of a new option titled Developer options (on newer versions of Android, this option is listed on the System settings screen).

Select this option, and on the resulting screen, locate the USB debugging option as illustrated in Figure 6-4:

Figure 6-4

4.  Enable the USB debugging option and tap the Allow button when confirmation is requested.

The device is now configured to accept debugging connections from ADB on the development system over a USB connection. With the device connected, the *adb devices* command should now list the device as being available:

```
List of devices attached
R9WN80H2TWJ        device
```

If the device is listed as *offline* or *unauthorized*, go to the device display and check for the dialog shown in Figure 6-5 seeking permission to *Allow USB debugging*. Enable the checkbox next to the option that reads *Always allow from this computer* before clicking *OK*:

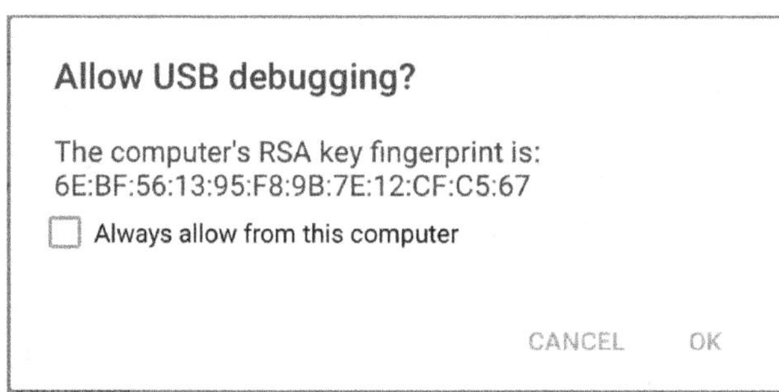


Figure 6-5

Repeating the *adb devices* command should now list the device as being ready:

```
C:\> adb devices
List of devices attached
HT4CTJT01906    device
```

If the device is not listed, execute the following commands to restart the ADB server:

```
C:\> adb kill-server
C:\> adb start-server
```

## 6.4 Running an App on the Device

Once the debug bridge to the device has been established, the physical device will be listed under Android Local Devices in the Visual Studio run target menu:

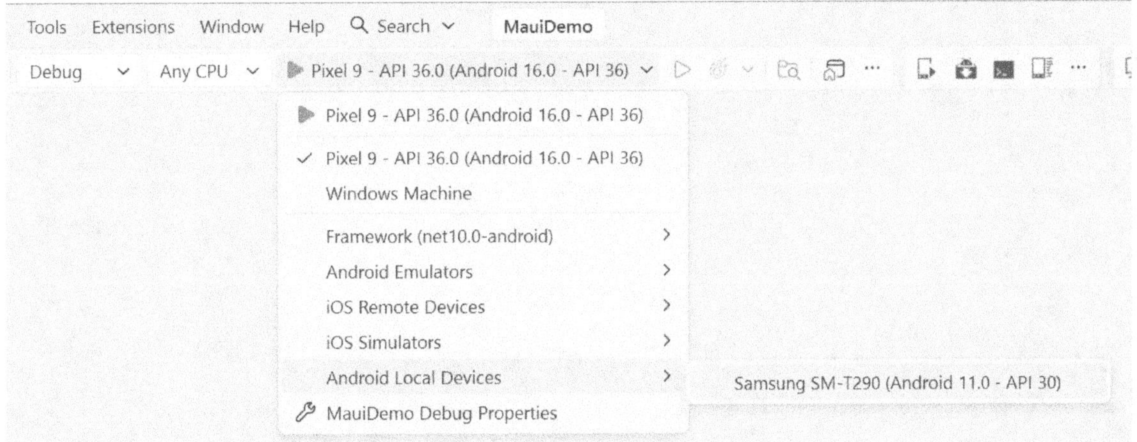


Figure 6-6

## 6.5 Summary

In this chapter, we explored how to test .NET MAUI applications on a physical Android device using the Android Debug Bridge (ADB). After introducing the role of ADB and its client, server, and device components, we configured the development environment by adding the Android SDK platform tools to the system path and verifying access to the adb command-line tool. We then enabled USB debugging on an Android device, established a connection to the development system, and confirmed that ADB recognized the device. Finally, we demonstrated how to deploy and run an application directly on the device from within Visual Studio, providing a more accurate real-world testing environment than an emulator alone.

# 7. Testing on iOS Simulators

It is difficult to imagine two more incompatible ecosystems than those belonging to Apple and Microsoft. These differences are reflected in the relative complexity of configuring a .NET MAUI app testing environment for iOS simulators and devices in comparison to Windows and Android testing. This chapter will explain how to test .NET MAUI apps on iOS simulators. While not necessarily difficult, this is a multi-step process that requires Xcode running on a macOS system and the Visual Studio Pair to Mac feature.

This chapter assumes that you have an Apple ID and access to a Mac.

## 7.1 Preparing the Mac for Remote Testing

Testing an app on an iOS simulator involves providing Visual Studio running on Windows with remote access to the Xcode environment on the Mac, which, in turn, requires installation of the Mono for macOS package, which can be downloaded from the following web page:

*https://www.mono-project.com/download/stable/#download-mac*

Once the Mono for macOS package has been installed on the Mac, open the macOS App Store and install the latest version of Xcode. The first time Xcode runs, you may be prompted to install additional components. Follow these steps, entering your username and password when prompted.

Once Xcode has loaded, and assuming this is the first time you have used Xcode on this system, you will be presented with the *Welcome* screen from which you are ready to proceed:

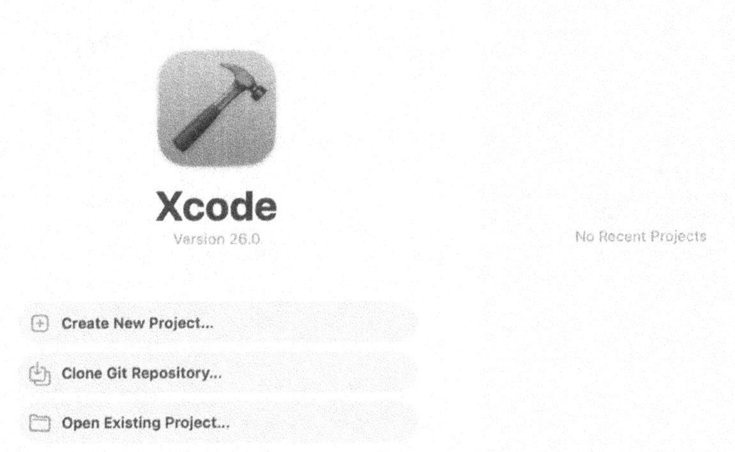


Figure 7-1

Testing on iOS Simulators

Select the *Xcode -> Settings…* menu option followed by the *Apple Accounts* entry in the navigation panel. On the Apple Accounts screen, click on the *Add Apple Account…* button highlighted in Figure 7-2, and enter your Apple ID and password to add the account:

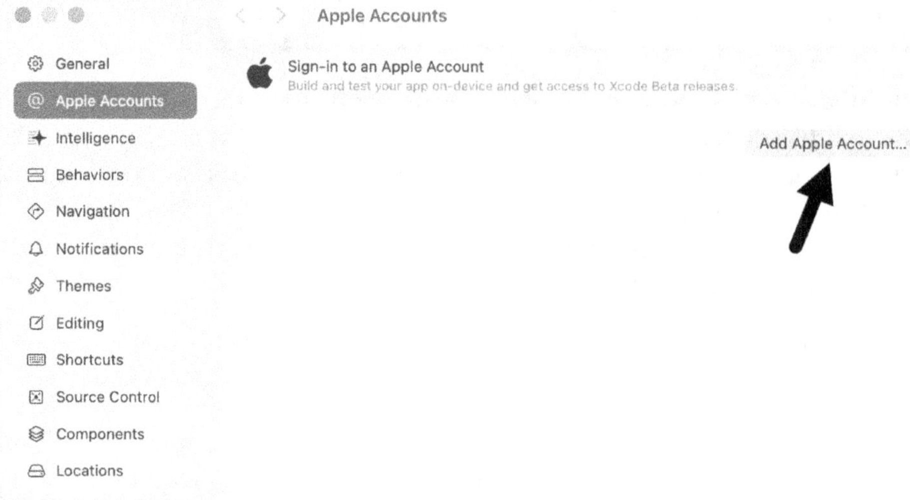

Figure 7-2

Finally, open the macOS System Settings app and navigate to the *General -> Sharing* screen. Scroll down to the Advanced section and enable the Remote Login option as illustrated in Figure 7-3:

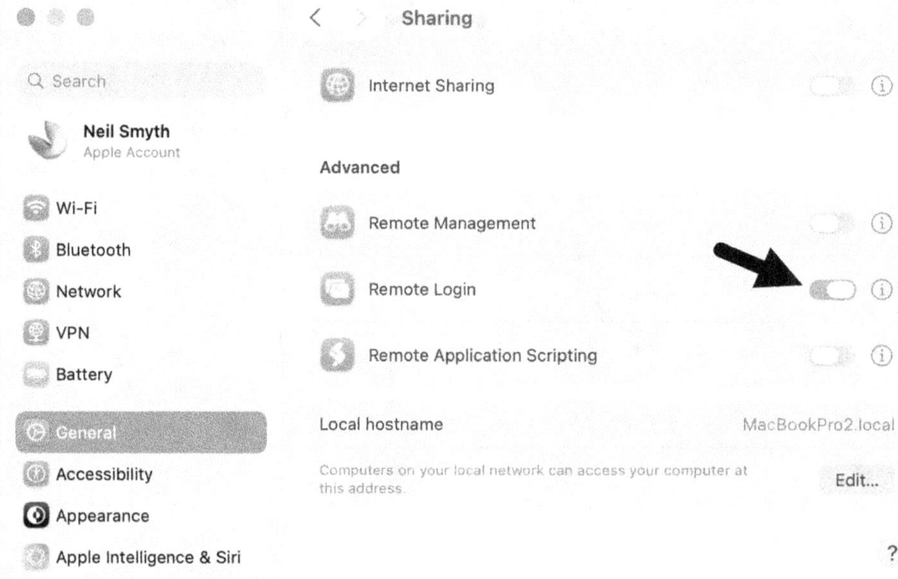

Figure 7-3

Click the information icon to the right of the Remote Login switch to display the remote settings panel shown in Figure 7-4. In the settings panel, enable the option to allow full disk access for remote users (marked A), set the menu marked B to *Only these users*, and click the '+' button (C) to add your account to the list of allowed remote users:

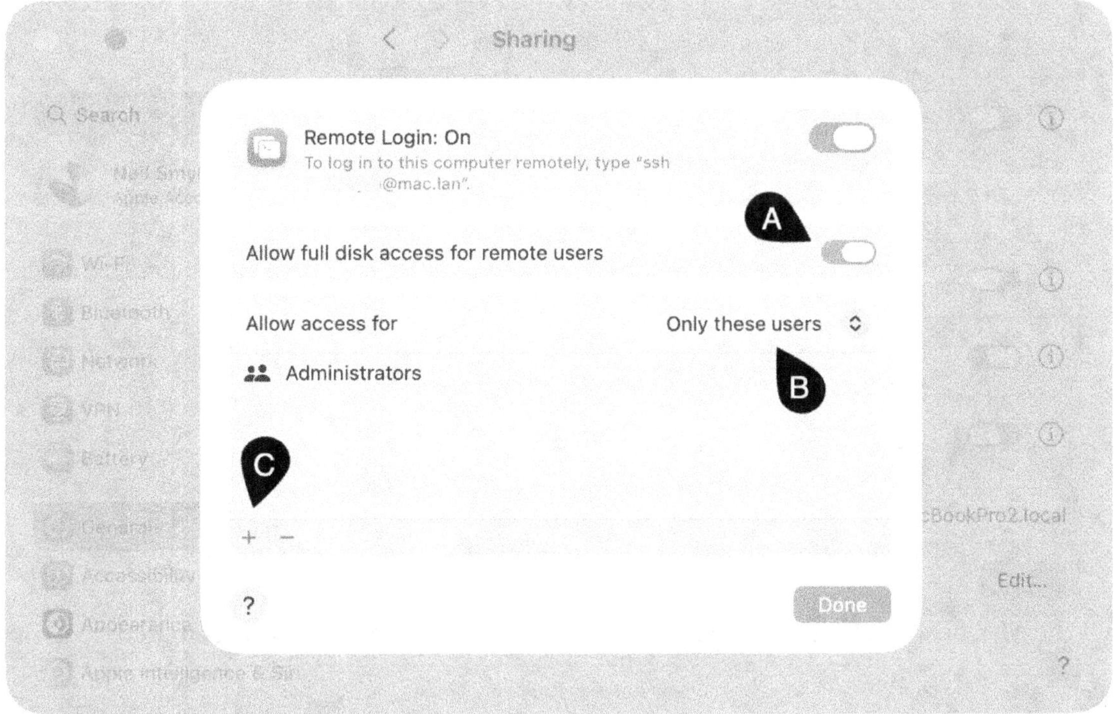

Figure 7-4

Click the Done button and close the System Settings app before proceeding.

## 7.2 Pairing to the Mac

Launch Visual Studio on Windows and open the MauiDemo project. Use the *Tools -> iOS -> Pair to Mac* menu option, or the toolbar button highlighted below, to display the Pair to Mac dialog:

Figure 7-5

Visual Studio will scan the network for the Mac build host and list it in the Pair to Mac dialog as illustrated in Figure 7-6:

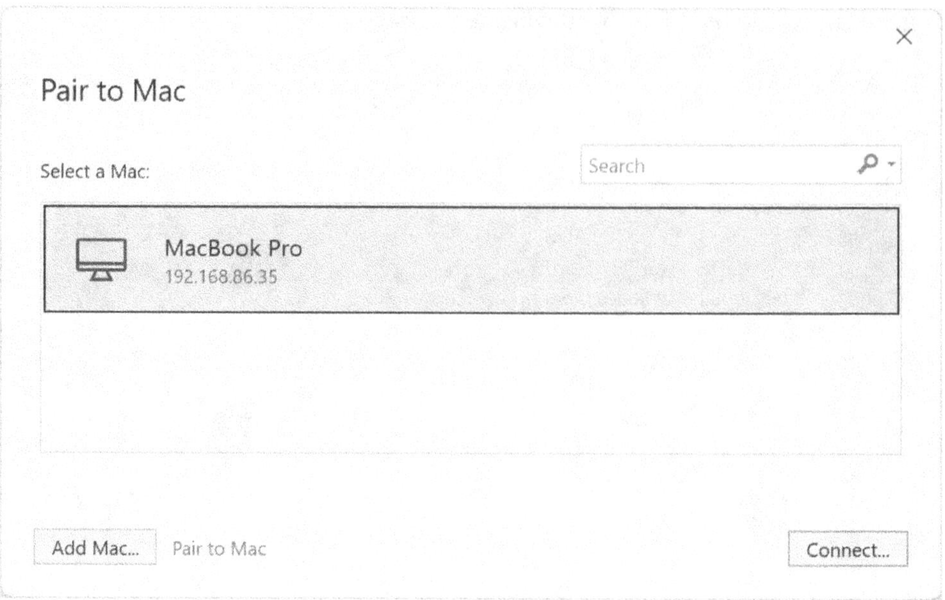

Figure 7-6

Select the Mac host, click the Connect button, and log in using your Mac account credentials:

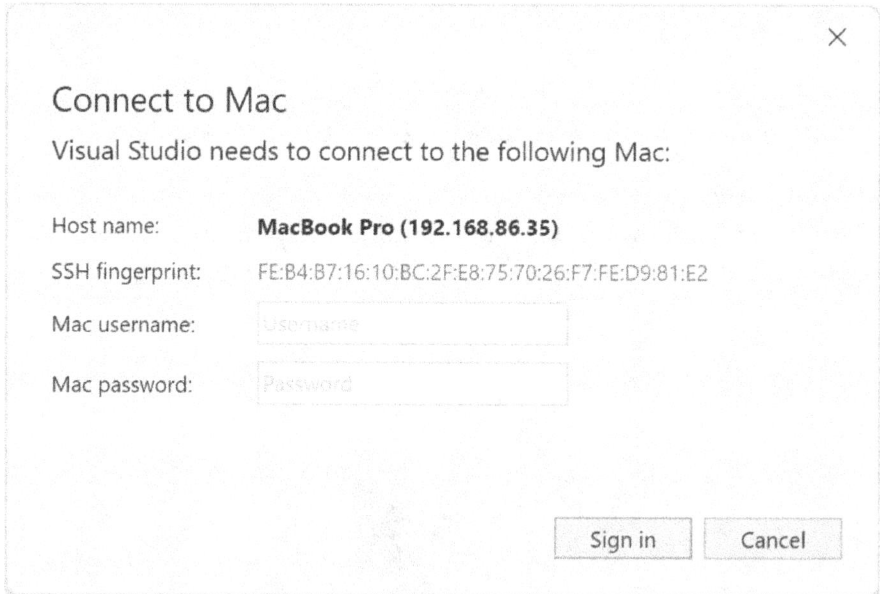

Figure 7-7

After entering your account details, click the *Sign in* button and wait while Visual Studio establishes the connection and installs the device toolkit onto the remote Mac system:

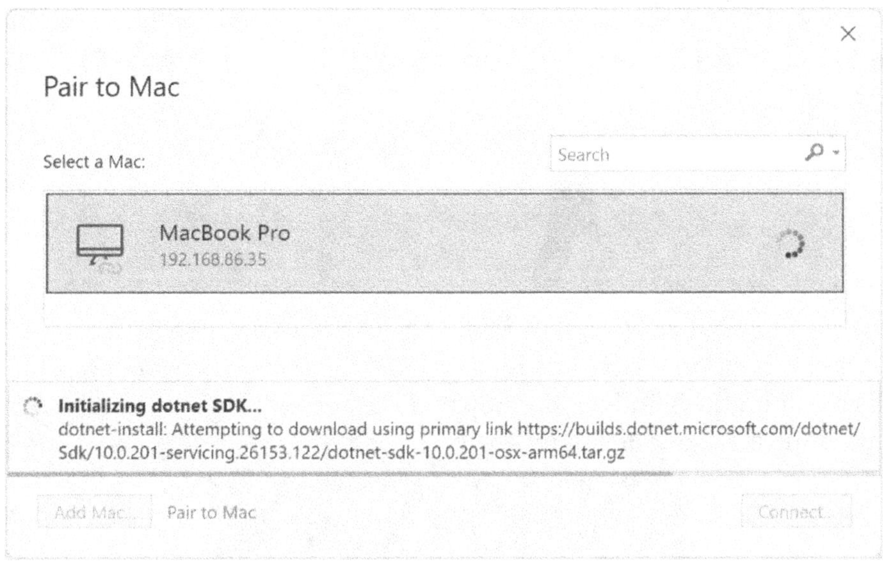

Figure 7-8

When the Mac has been paired successfully, close the Pair to Mac dialog.

## 7.3 Running the App on the iOS Simulator

To build and run the app on the iOS simulator, begin by opening the run target menu in the Visual Studio toolbar and selecting a device from the iOS Simulators sub-menu, as shown in Figure 7-9:

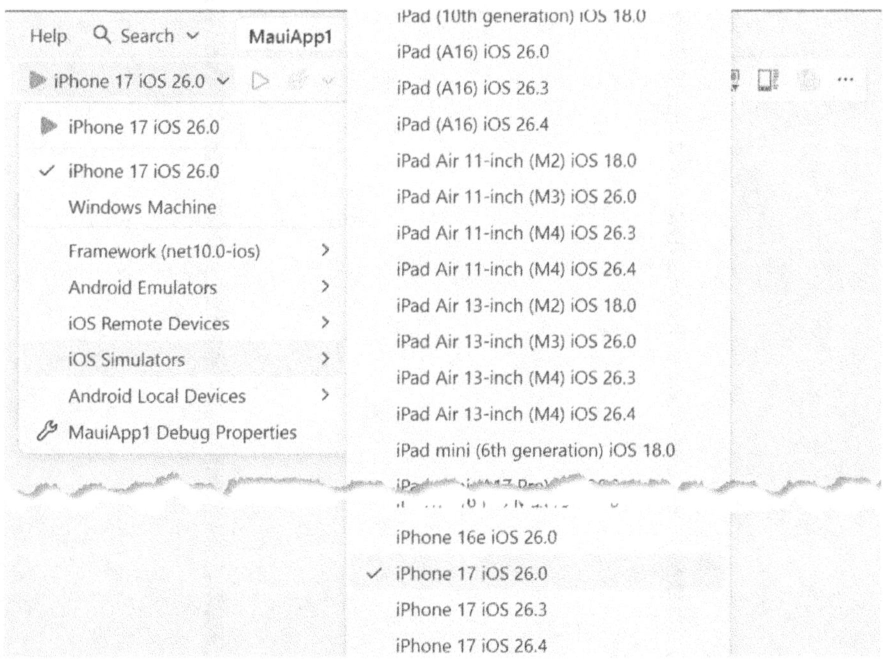

Figure 7-9

After selecting a simulator from the list, click the run button to build and launch the app:

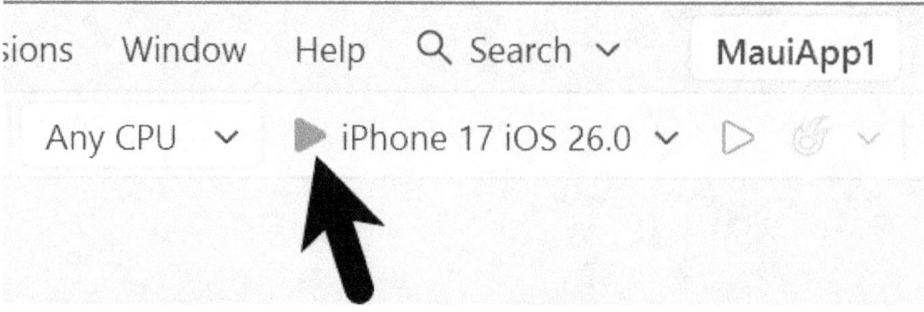


Figure 7-10

Wait while the app is built on the remote Mac system. Assuming there are no problems, the iOS simulator will appear on the Windows desktop and the app will launch (refer to the next section if the build fails with an Xcode version mismatch error):

Figure 7-11

## 7.4 Xcode Version Mismatch

Each .NET for iOS release requires a specific version of Xcode for building and deploying iOS apps. If the currently installed Xcode version is not compatible, the build will fail with an error similar to the following:

```
This version of .NET for iOS (26.2.10217) requires Xcode 26.2. The
current version of Xcode is 26.4. Either install Xcode 26.2, or use a
different version of .NET for iOS. See https://aka.ms/xcode-requirement
for more information.
```

In the above case, the installed version of Xcode (26.4) is too recent for compatibility with the current version of .NET for iOS which requires Xcode 26.2. If you encounter this problem, you can download a compatible version of Xcode from the Apple Developer website. Navigate to the following page in a browser and sign in using your Apple ID:

*https://developer.apple.com/download/all/?q=xcode*

On the download page, search for and download the compatible Xcode version. Uninstall the incompatible Xcode version before installing the downloaded Xcode package. Return to Visual Studio and use the Pair to Mac dialog to disconnect and reconnect to the Mac, then try rebuilding the app.

## 7.5 Summary

In this chapter, we explored how to configure a Windows-based development environment to test .NET MAUI applications on the iOS simulator. After preparing a Mac with Mono and Xcode, and configuring remote access and Apple account settings, we used Visual Studio's Pair to Mac feature to establish a connection between the Windows system and the macOS build host. With this connection in place, we selected an iOS simulator from within Visual Studio and deployed the app to run remotely on the Mac. We also addressed potential Xcode version compatibility issues and how to resolve them. With this setup complete, you can build and test .NET MAUI applications on iOS simulators directly from Visual Studio on Windows.

# 8. Testing on iOS Devices

In the previous chapter, we configured the development environment to build and run a .NET MAUI application on an iOS simulator using a paired Mac. While the simulator provides a fast and convenient way to test layout and general functionality, it does not fully replicate the behavior of a real device. Hardware features such as camera access, biometric authentication, device performance, and certain system integrations can only be tested accurately on physical hardware.

For this reason, testing on a real iPhone or iPad is an essential step in the development process. Although this process builds on the simulator setup, additional configuration is required to allow the application to be signed and installed on a physical device. In particular, the workflow described in this chapter requires an active paid Apple Developer Program membership to generate an App Store Connect API key for code signing.

With these prerequisites in place, this chapter explains how to prepare the device, configure signing using an App Store Connect API key, and deploy a .NET MAUI application directly from Visual Studio.

## 8.1 Preparing the Mac and Device

Before deploying to a physical device, ensure that the Mac used for remote builds is correctly configured. Xcode must be installed and launched at least once so that all required components are available. In addition, your Apple developer account must already be configured within Xcode.

Next, connect the iPhone or iPad to the Mac using a USB cable. When prompted on the device, tap the Trust option and enter the device passcode. This step establishes a trusted connection between the device and the Mac.

To confirm that the device is available, open Xcode on the Mac and select the *Window -> Devices and Simulators* menu option. The connected device should appear in the list:

Figure 8-1

Testing on iOS Devices

If the device is not listed, check the cable connection and ensure that the device is unlocked.

At this stage, the Mac is able to communicate with the device and is ready to perform builds and deployments.

## 8.2 Understanding the Role of the App Store Connect API Key

Unlike Android, iOS requires applications to be digitally signed before they can be installed on a device. This signing process relies on certificates and provisioning profiles associated with your Apple developer account.

In recent versions of Visual Studio, access to these resources is handled via an App Store Connect API key rather than entering Apple ID credentials directly. The API key allows Visual Studio to communicate securely with Apple services to retrieve signing information, manage provisioning profiles, and associate the app with your developer team.

It is important to note that generating an App Store Connect API key requires an active paid Apple Developer Program membership. While it is possible to deploy apps to a physical device using a free Apple ID in some development workflows, the API key-based approach used by Visual Studio requires a registered developer account. If you do not have a paid membership, you will need to enroll in the Apple Developer Program before proceeding.

Although Visual Studio manages the configuration on the Windows side, the actual build and signing still occur on the paired Mac using Xcode. Visual Studio coordinates this process through the Pair to Mac connection.

## 8.3 Creating an App Store Connect API Key

Before configuring the project, an API key must be created within App Store Connect.

Open a web browser, navigate to the Apple Developer portal, sign in using your Apple developer account, and select the Users and Access link as highlighted in Figure 8-2:

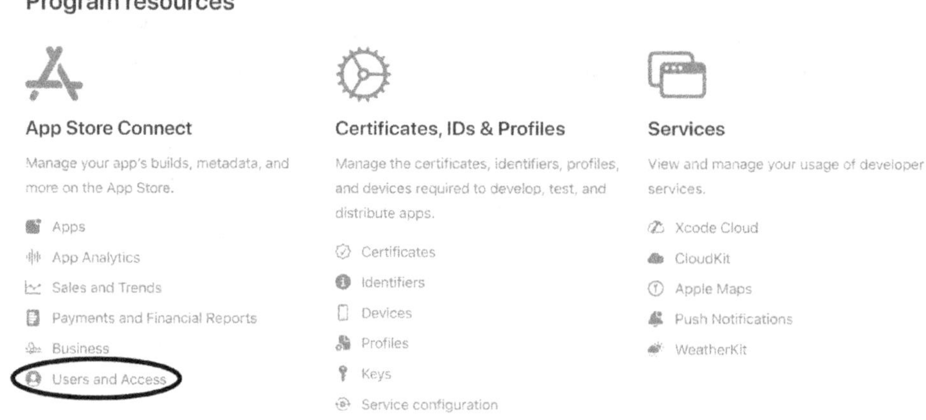


Figure 8-2

On the Users and Access screen, select the Integrations tab and click the Request Access button if you have not previously generated a key:

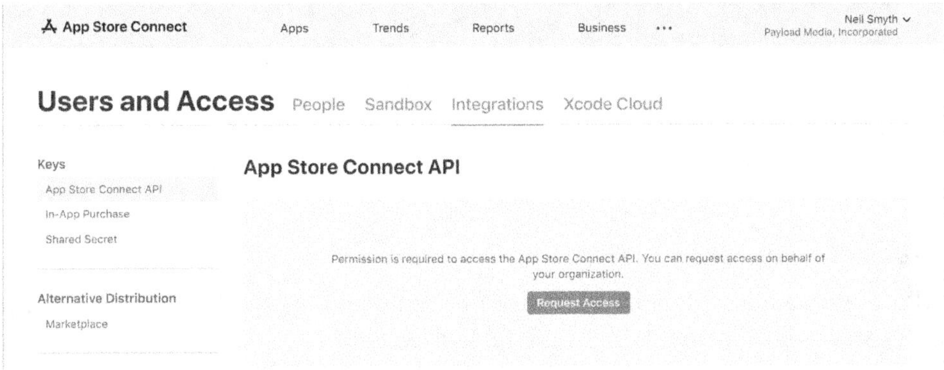

Figure 8-3

Once access has been granted, click the Generate API Key button on the Team Keys panel:

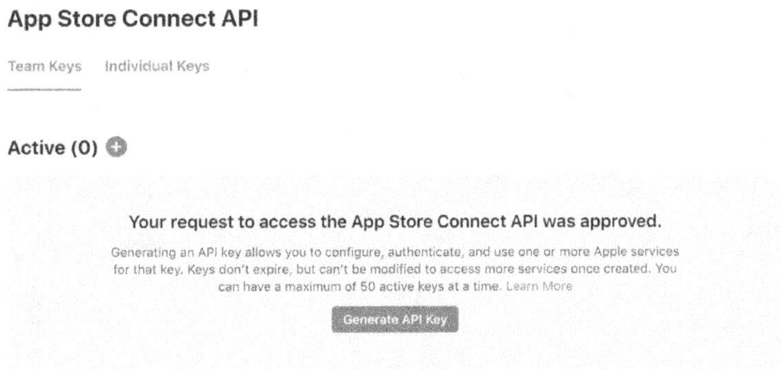

Figure 8-4

In the resulting dialog, provide a descriptive name for the key and add the Developer role in the Access field:

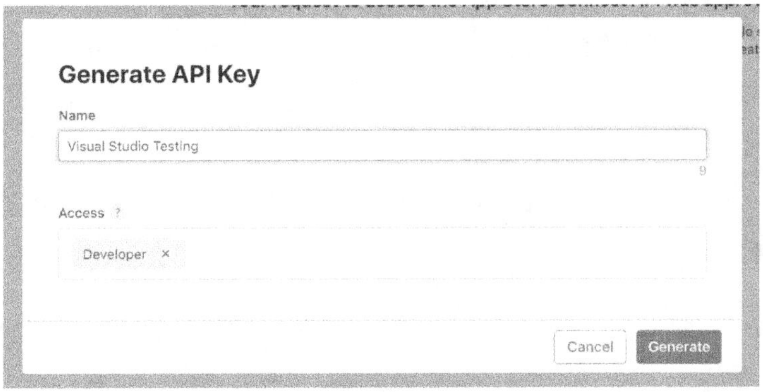

Figure 8-5

Click the Generate button to create the key, which will appear in the Team Keys panel. Click Download and save the P8 key file to your local filesystem. This file is only available for download once and must be stored securely. We will also need to enter the Issuer ID and Key ID values into

Visual Studio, so keep the current page open in the browser until later:

Figure 8-6

## 8.4 Configuring Visual Studio

With the API key created, start Visual Studio on Windows, open the MauiDemo project, and ensure that the Mac is connected using the Pair to Mac feature.

Next, select the *Tools -> Options* menu option and navigate to *All Settings -> .NET MAUI -> Apple -> Accounts*:

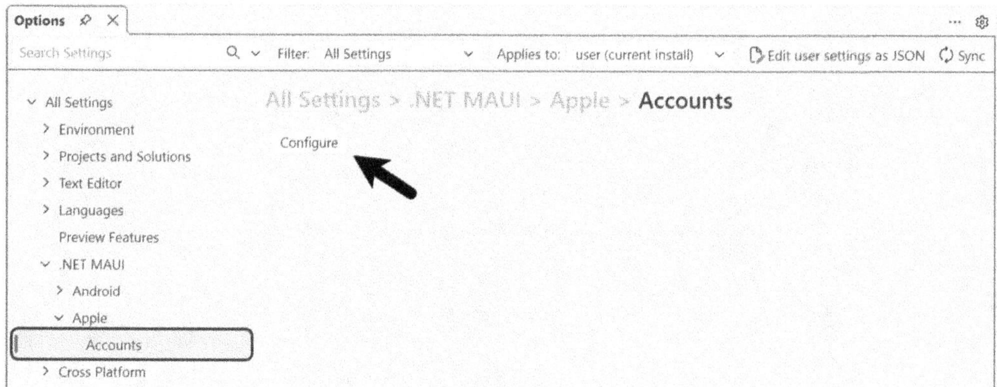

Figure 8-7

Click the Configure button to display the Apple Developer Accounts dialog:

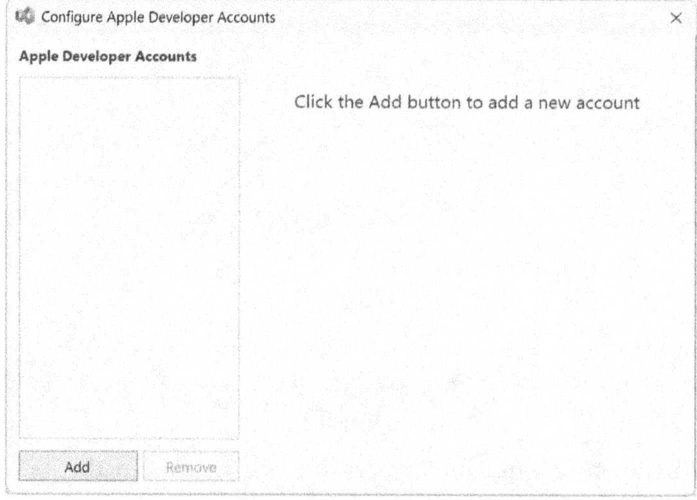

Figure 8-8

Click the Add button, then, when prompted, provide the Key ID and Issuer ID, and use the Browse button to locate and select the .p8 API key file before closing the dialog.

At this point, Visual Studio has access to the necessary signing information and can coordinate with the Mac to build and sign the application.

## 8.5 Selecting the Physical Device

With the project configured and the device connected to the Mac, the device will appear as a deployment target within the Visual Studio target menu under iOS Remote Devices:

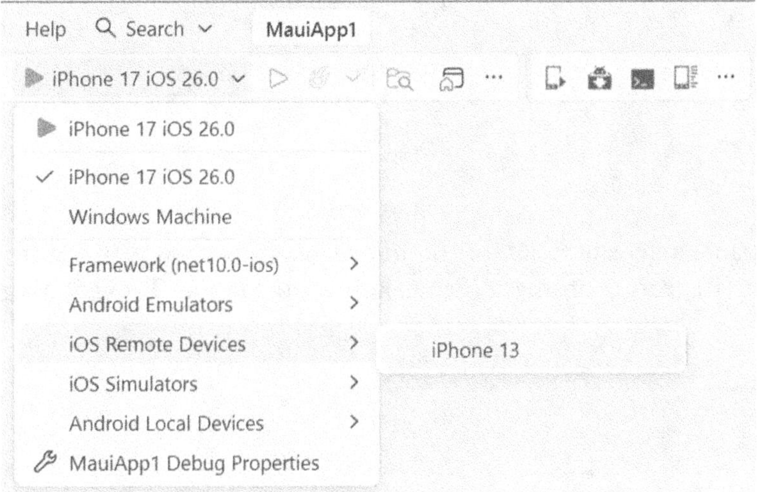

Figure 8-9

Select the device as the run target before proceeding.

## 8.6 Running the Application on the Device

Click the run button to begin the build and deployment process. The application will be compiled on the Mac using Xcode, signed using the provisioning profile associated with your developer account, and then installed on the connected device. Once deployment is complete, the app will launch automatically on the device.

## 8.7 Troubleshooting

There are several reasons why the project may fail to build and deploy on the physical device. If you have previously run the app on an iOS simulator, you may encounter the following error:

```
Automatic Provisioning is enabled but no account was selected. Please
select a team or switch to Manual Provisioning from the iOS Bundle
Signing page.
```

To resolve this problem, open the Solution Explorer, right-click on the MauiDemo entry, and select the *Properties...* menu option, as shown in Figure 8-10:

# Testing on iOS Devices

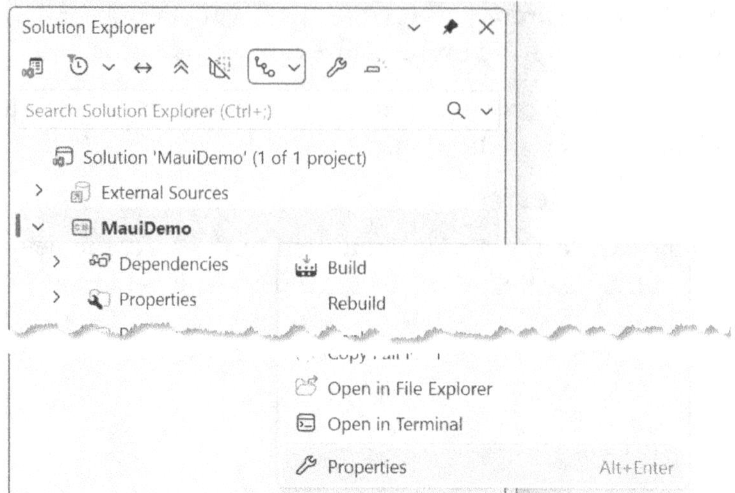

Figure 8-10

In the Properties panel, navigate to *iOS -> Bundle Signing* (marked A in Figure 8-11) and change the Scheme menu (B) from Automatic Provisioning to Manual Provisioning, then restart the build:

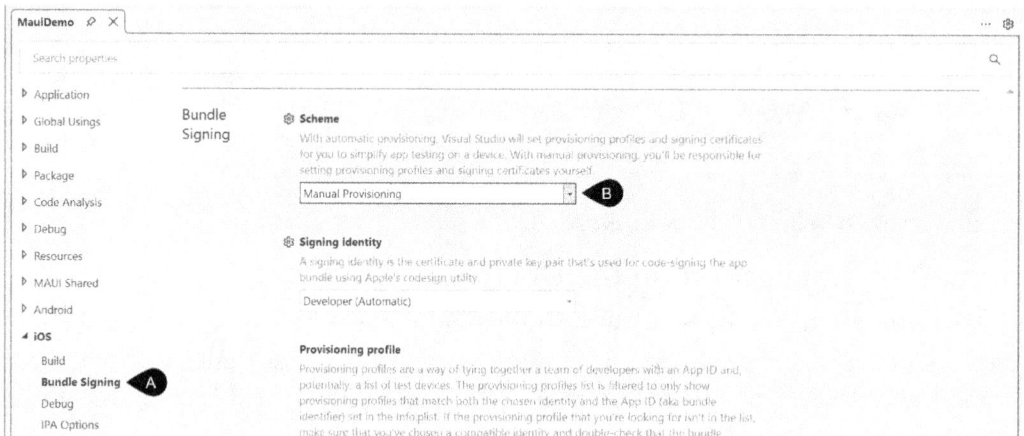

Figure 8-11

If you have previously run the app on an iOS simulator, you may encounter the following error:

```
/obj/Debug/net10.0-ios/iossimulator-arm64/nativelibraries/aot-output/
arm64/System.Private.CoreLib.dll.o) built for 'iOS-simulator'
clang++: error: linker command failed with exit code 1 (use -v to see
invocation)
```

To correct this issue, right-click on the MauiDemo entry and select the Edit Project File menu option. When the project file loads into the editor, delete the following lines before rebuilding the app:

```
<PropertyGroup Condition="$([MSBuild]::GetTargetPlatformIdentifier('$(Targ
etFramework)')) == 'ios'">
    <RuntimeIdentifier>ios-arm64</RuntimeIdentifier>
```

```
</PropertyGroup>
```

## 8.8 Summary

In this chapter, we configured a .NET MAUI application to run on a physical iOS device by preparing the Mac and the device, setting up signing with an App Store Connect API key, and deploying the app via the Pair to Mac connection. By building and signing on the Mac and installing directly onto the device, we enabled real-world testing that more accurately reflects how the application will behave in production.

# 9. A Guided Tour of Visual Studio

Before beginning development with .NET MAUI and C# Markup, it is important to become familiar with the Visual Studio development environment. Visual Studio provides a comprehensive set of tools for writing, building, debugging, and managing applications. While the interface may appear complex at first, it is organized into clearly defined areas, each with a specific purpose.

In this chapter, we will take a guided tour of the main components of the Visual Studio user interface and explore how they are used during development. By the end of the chapter, you will have a clear understanding of how to navigate the environment and where to find the tools you need when building your applications.

## 9.1 The Main Window Layout

The Visual Studio environment is centered around the code editor (marked A in Figure 9-1), which occupies the largest portion of the screen. Surrounding the editor are panels known as tool windows, each providing access to a specific aspect of the development process.

Across the top of the window is the menu bar and toolbar (B), which provide access to commands and commonly used actions such as building and running the application. Along the sides are tool windows, including Solution Explorer (C) and Properties, while additional windows can be displayed or hidden as needed.

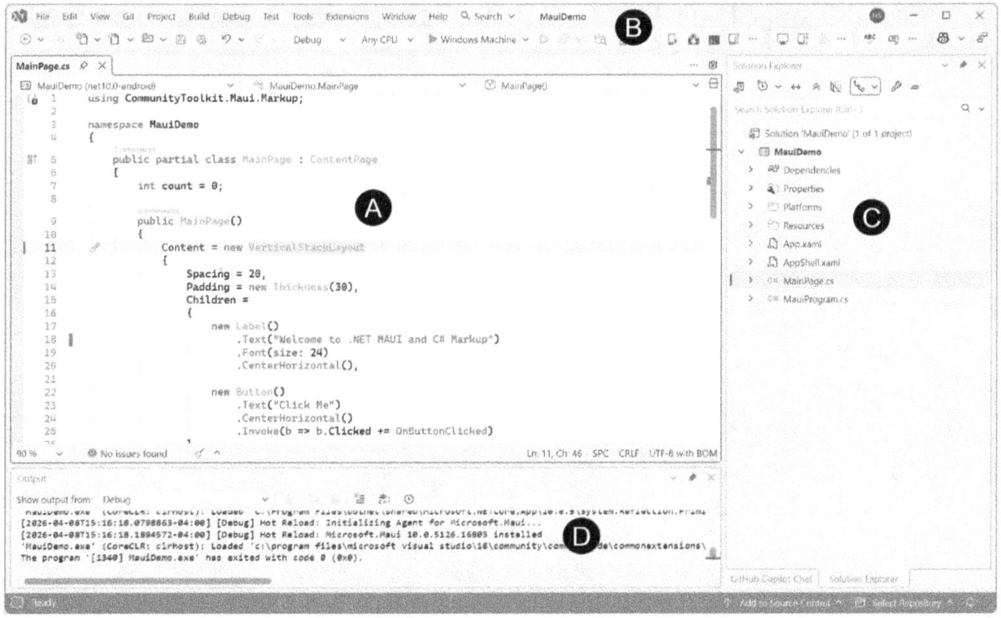

Figure 9-1

The above figure illustrates the primary regions of the Visual Studio workspace. Although the exact arrangement may vary depending on your configuration, the core components remain the same.

## 9.2 The Code Editor

The code editor is where application source code is written and modified. It supports syntax highlighting, automatic formatting, and real-time error detection. As you type, Visual Studio provides suggestions through IntelliSense, allowing you to insert code elements and reduce typing errors quickly.

Multiple files can be opened simultaneously, each appearing as a tab, allowing you to switch easily between different parts of the project, as shown in Figure 9-2:

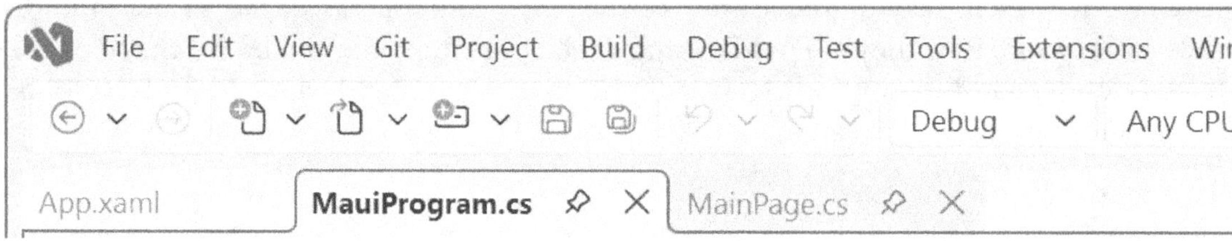

Figure 9-2

## 9.3 Solution Explorer

The Solution Explorer window provides a structured view of the files and folders that make up the project. It allows you to navigate the project hierarchy, open files, and manage resources. New files and folders can also be added directly from this window, making it the primary tool for managing project structure:

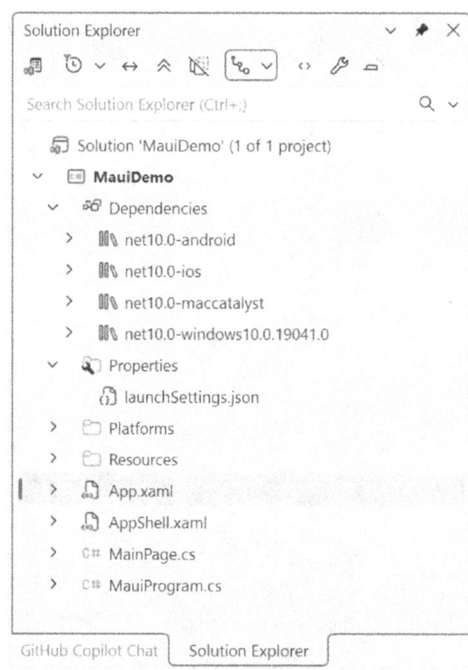

Figure 9-3

## 9.4 The Toolbar and Run Controls

The toolbar (B in Figure 9-1) provides quick access to commonly used commands, including building and running the application.

The run target selector shown in Figure 9-4 below lets you choose where the application will be deployed, such as an Android emulator, iOS simulator, or a physical device. Once selected, the run button builds and launches the app:

Figure 9-4

## 9.5 Output and Error Windows

The Output window (marked D in Figure 9-1) displays detailed information about build and deployment processes, while the Error List highlights issues detected in the code:

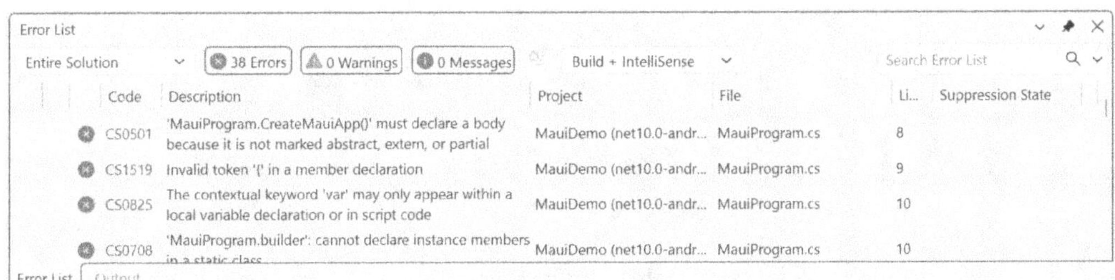

| | Code | Description | Project | File | Li... | Suppression State |
|---|---|---|---|---|---|---|
| ⊗ | CS0501 | 'MauiProgram.CreateMauiApp()' must declare a body because it is not marked abstract, extern, or partial | MauiDemo (net10.0-andr... | MauiProgram.cs | 8 | |
| ⊗ | CS1519 | Invalid token '(' in a member declaration | MauiDemo (net10.0-andr... | MauiProgram.cs | 9 | |
| ⊗ | CS0825 | The contextual keyword 'var' may only appear within a local variable declaration or in script code | MauiDemo (net10.0-andr... | MauiProgram.cs | 10 | |
| ⊗ | CS0708 | 'MauiProgram.builder': cannot declare instance members in a static class | MauiDemo (net10.0-andr... | MauiProgram.cs | 10 | |

Figure 9-5

Selecting an error navigates directly to the corresponding line, making it easier to diagnose and fix problems.

## 9.6 Debugging Tools

Visual Studio includes powerful debugging tools that allow you to pause execution, inspect variables, and step through code.

Breakpoints can be set in the editor to pause execution at specific lines. While paused, you can examine the application state and track down issues.

## 9.7 Using Copilot in Visual Studio

Visual Studio includes integrated AI assistance through GitHub Copilot, which can significantly improve productivity when writing code.

Copilot works directly within the code editor and provides suggestions as you type. These suggestions may include entire lines of code, method implementations, or even complete UI layouts, depending on the context.

As you write code, Copilot analyzes the current context and offers suggestions inline. Pressing the appropriate key accepts the suggestion, allowing you to insert code quickly.

Copilot can also assist with more complex tasks, such as generating methods, explaining existing code, or suggesting improvements. Select the tab indicated in Figure 9-6 below to display the Copilot window, where you can interact with the AI assistant:

Figure 9-6

## 9.8 Customizing the Environment

Visual Studio allows the layout and appearance of the interface to be customized. Tool windows can be moved, resized, or hidden, enabling you to tailor the workspace to your preferences. To move a window, click on the title bar or tab and drag it to the desired location. When the location highlights, drop the window into place and click and drag the dividers between the windows to adjust the relative window sizes.

To change the theme, select an option from the *Tools -> Theme* and *Tools -> Editor Theme* menus, and make font and color changes by selecting the *Tools -> Options* menu item and navigating to the *All Settings -> Environment -> Visual Experience -> Fonts* category in the navigation panel.

## 9.9 Summary

In this chapter, we explored the main components of the Visual Studio user interface, including the code editor, tool windows, and debugging tools. We also introduced GitHub Copilot to assist with code generation. With an understanding of these features, you are now ready to navigate the environment and begin building applications.

# 10. Working with the Visual Studio Code Editor

At the heart of the Visual Studio development environment is the code editor. This is where application logic is written, modified, and refined throughout the development process. While Visual Studio provides many supporting tools, the editor is where you will spend most of your time.

The editor is far more than a simple text editing tool. It includes features designed to help you write code efficiently, avoid errors, and perform common tasks with minimal effort. In this chapter, we will explore how to use the editor effectively, including navigating files, editing multiple lines, refactoring code, and leveraging productivity features such as IntelliSense and search tools.

## 10.1 Opening and Navigating Files

Files are typically opened from the Solution Explorer window by double-clicking the file name. Once opened, the file appears as a tab in the editor. Multiple files can be opened at the same time, allowing you to switch between them by clicking the corresponding tabs.

To navigate within a file, you can scroll using the mouse or keyboard. Visual Studio also provides a quick way to jump to specific locations. Pressing Ctrl+G opens the Go To Line dialog, where you can enter a line number and move directly to that location. Alternatively, pressing Ctrl+T (or Ctrl+,) allows you to search for files, classes, or methods and jump directly to them.

## 10.2 Using IntelliSense

As you type code, Visual Studio displays suggestions through IntelliSense. To use IntelliSense, begin typing a class or method name. A list of matching options will appear as shown in Figure 10-1 from which to make a selection:

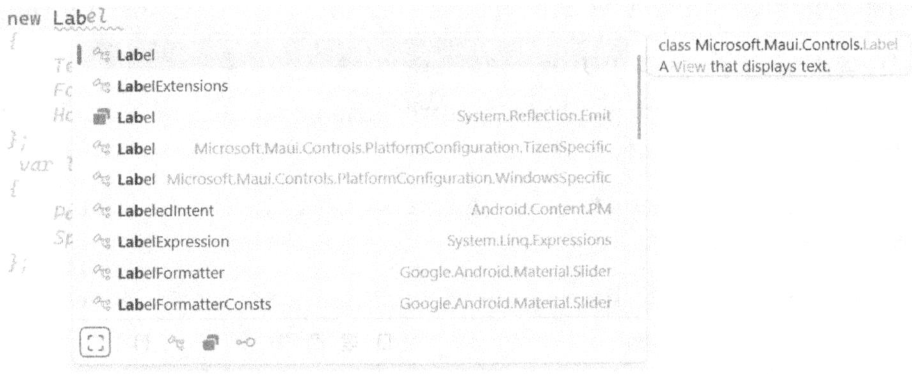


Figure 10-1

Working with the Visual Studio Code Editor

You can use the arrow keys to select an item and press Enter to insert it into the code, or scroll through the options with the mouse and click to make a selection.

Similarly, IntelliSense will infer potential code completions based on your initial typing and the code context. In Figure 10-2, for example, typing 'var layout' in a page declaration might cause IntelliSense to suggest a VerticalStackLayout instance including spacing and padding:

```
3    ∨ namespace LayoutDemo
4        {
            14 references
5    ∨       public partial class MainPage : ContentPage
6            {
                0 references
7    ∨           public MainPage()
8                {
9
10→|                  var layout = new VerticalStackLayout
                      {
                          Padding = 20,
                          Spacing = 10
                      };
11
```

Figure 10-2

## 10.3 Editing Multiple Lines

When working with repetitive code, it is often helpful to edit multiple lines simultaneously. Visual Studio provides several ways to achieve this.

One approach is to use multiple cursors. Hold down the Ctrl +Alt keys and left-click at different locations in the editor to place additional cursors. Once multiple cursors are active, typing will update all selected lines simultaneously.

Another method is to use column (block) selection. Hold down the Alt key and drag the mouse vertically to select a rectangular block of text. Any changes made will apply across all selected lines.

For example, if you have several Label elements and want to add the same property to each, you can place cursors on each line and type the change once instead of repeating it manually.

## 10.4 Commenting and Uncommenting Code

During development, it is often useful to temporarily disable sections of code. This can be done by commenting out lines.

To comment selected lines, highlight the code and press Ctrl+K, Ctrl+C. To remove the comments, press Ctrl+K, Ctrl+U.

This is particularly useful when testing alternative implementations or isolating issues.

## 10.5 Finding and Replacing Text

Visual Studio's code editor provides tools for locating and modifying text. To search within the current file, press Ctrl+F and enter the text to find. Matches will be highlighted in the editor. To replace matched text within the current file, press Ctrl+H.

To search across the entire project, press Ctrl+Shift+F and enter the search criteria in the Find and Replace dialog shown in Figure 10-3:

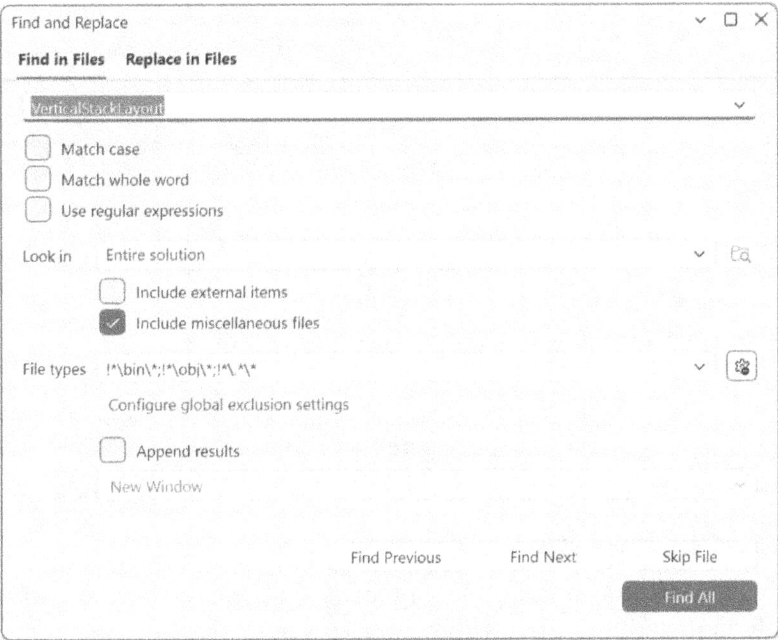


Figure 10-3

This allows you to find and replace individual occurrences or all matches within a file or project.

## 10.6 Refactoring Code

Refactoring allows you to improve the structure of your code without changing its behavior. Visual Studio provides built-in tools to perform these operations safely.

To refactor code, place the cursor on a variable, method, or class name and press Ctrl+R, Ctrl+R to rename it. Visual Studio will automatically update all references.

For example, if you rename a variable used in multiple places, all occurrences will be updated consistently.

You can also extract sections of code into a new method. Highlight the code you want to extract, right-click, and select the *Refactor and Quick Actions...* menu option, and choose whether to extract the selected code as a method or local function:

```
        count++;

        if (sender is Button button)
        {
            if (count == 1)
                button.Text = $"Clicked {count} time";
            else
                button.Text = $"Clicked {count} times";
        }
```

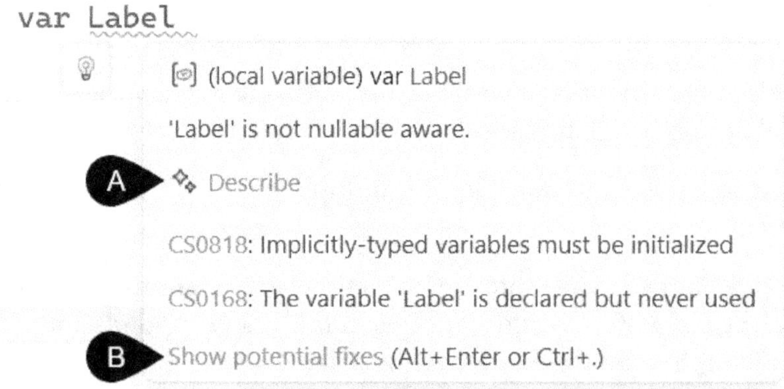


Figure 10-4

Visual Studio will extract the selected code and replace it with a call to the new method or function.

## 10.7 Real-Time Error Detection

As you write code, Visual Studio continuously analyzes it for errors and warnings. Issues are highlighted directly in the editor, often with colored underlines.

Hovering over an error displays a message describing the problem, along with suggestions for resolving it. In many cases, Visual Studio can automatically fix issues through quick actions. In Figure 10-5, for example, the editor has detected a syntax error and offers some actions:



Figure 10-5

Clicking the Describe option (A) will provide detailed information about the problem, while the option to show fixes (B) will display a dialog similar to Figure 10-6:

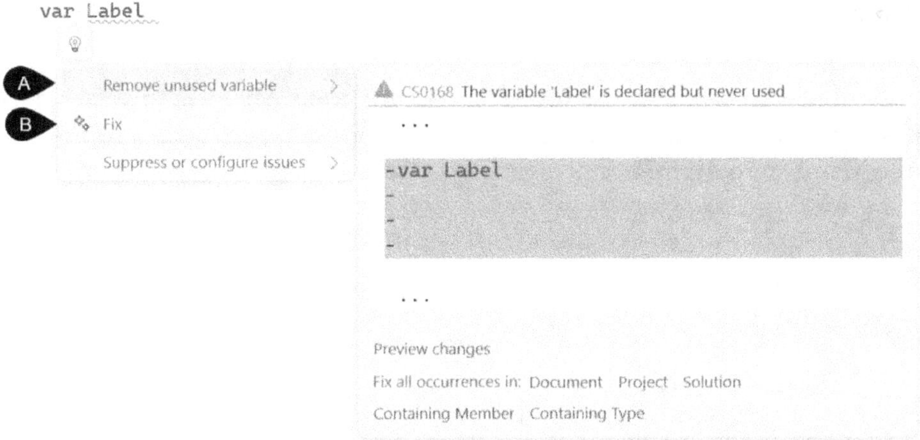

Figure 10-6

In the above example, the editor provides the option to remove the partially declared variable (marked A in Figure 10-6). Alternatively, the Fix option (B) will use Copilot to analyze the problems and suggest a resolution.

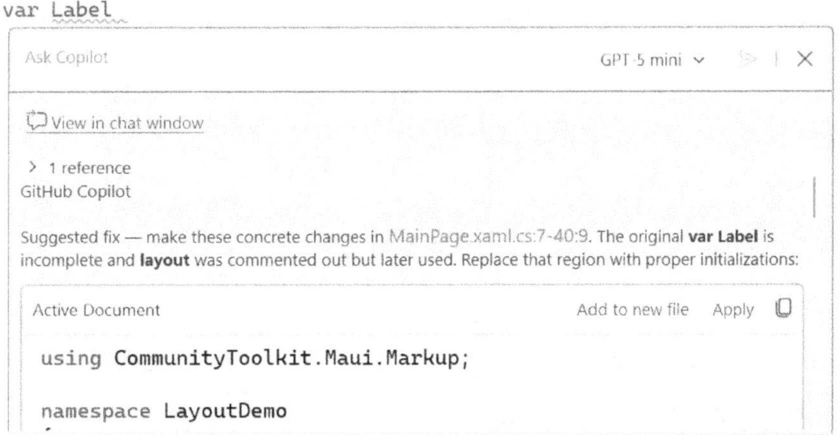

Figure 10-7

This real-time feedback helps you identify and correct problems early in the development process.

## 10.8 Formatting Code

Maintaining consistent formatting improves readability. Visual Studio can automatically format code for you. To format the entire document, press Ctrl+K, Ctrl+D. To format a selected block of code, press Ctrl+K, Ctrl+F. This ensures consistent indentation and spacing throughout your code.

## 10.9 Navigating Between Code Elements

When working in larger files, it is often necessary to move quickly between methods, variables, and classes.

You can use the navigation bar at the top of the editor to select a class, variable, or method. In Figure 10-8, for example, the navigation bar is providing direct access to the methods and variables in the MauiDemo *MainPage.cs* file:

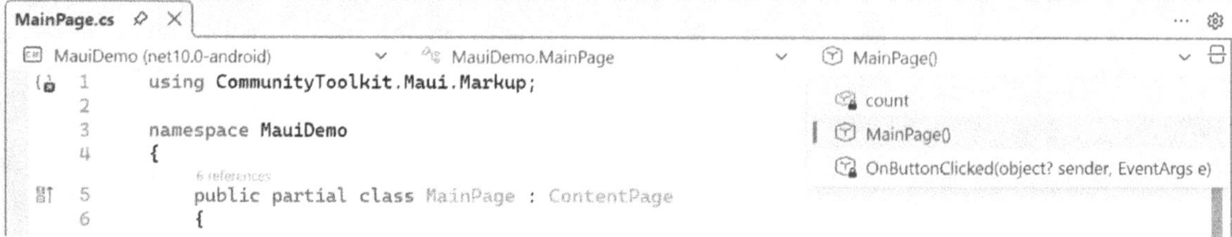

Figure 10-8

Alternatively, right-click on a symbol and select Go To Definition, or press F12 to jump directly to its declaration. To return to the previous location, press Ctrl+-.

## 10.10 Splitting the Editor

To view two sections of the same file at once, you can split the editor window by clicking and dragging the splitter control located at the top right of the scroll bar, as highlighted in Figure 10-9:

Figure 10-9

This editor feature is useful when working with long files or comparing different sections of code.

## 10.11 Keyboard Shortcuts Reference

As you become more familiar with the Visual Studio code editor, using keyboard shortcuts can significantly improve your productivity. Many common tasks can be performed more quickly from the keyboard than by navigating menus or using the mouse.

The following table lists some of the most frequently used shortcuts when working in the code editor. While it is not necessary to memorize all of them immediately, becoming comfortable with a small subset will greatly speed up your workflow over time.

| Action | Shortcut | Description |
| --- | --- | --- |
| Go to line | Ctrl + G | Navigate directly to a specified line number |

| Search in file | Ctrl + F | Find text within the current file |
|---|---|---|
| Search in solution | Ctrl + Shift + F | Search across all files in the project |
| Replace text | Ctrl + H | Find and replace text in the current file |
| Trigger IntelliSense | Ctrl + Space | Display code completion suggestions |
| Quick Actions | Ctrl + . | Open suggested fixes and refactorings |
| Go to definition | F12 | Navigate to the definition of a symbol |
| Go back | Ctrl + - | Return to the previous cursor location |
| Rename symbol | Ctrl + R, Ctrl + R | Rename a variable, method, or class |
| Format document | Ctrl + K, Ctrl + D | Format the entire file |
| Format selection | Ctrl + K, Ctrl + F | Format selected code |
| Comment selection | Ctrl + K, Ctrl + C | Comment selected lines |
| Uncomment selection | Ctrl + K, Ctrl + U | Remove comments from selected lines |
| Multi-cursor editing | Alt + Click | Place multiple cursors for simultaneous editing |
| Column selection | Alt + Drag | Select a vertical block of text |
| Go to file/symbol | Ctrl + T or Ctrl + , | Quickly navigate to files, classes, or members |
| Show error list | Ctrl + \ , Ctrl + E | Open the Error List window |

Table 10-1

## 10.12 Summary

In this chapter, we explored how to use the Visual Studio code editor to write and manage code efficiently. We covered navigation techniques, IntelliSense, multi-line editing, search and replace, and refactoring tools. By learning how to use these features effectively, you can work more quickly, reduce errors, and maintain clean, well-structured code in your C# Markup projects.

# 11. Working with Layouts

One of the first things every developer needs to understand in .NET MAUI is how to arrange controls on the screen. Layouts are the containers that define where your views appear and how they behave when the window resizes or the device orientation changes. In C# Markup, you can construct these same layouts directly in code using a fluent, expressive style. This chapter explores StackLayout, Grid, FlexLayout, and AbsoluteLayout.

## 11.1 Understanding View Hierarchies and Layouts in .NET MAUI

The pages of a .NET MAUI app are composed as hierarchical trees of individual views. Views are the basic building blocks of a user interface, including buttons, labels, and text input fields.

Each page contains a hierarchy of views that represent the page's UI layout. Views can be individual visual elements, such as labels or buttons, or containers that manage other views. The StackLayout view, for example, is designed to display child views in a vertical or horizontal orientation.

Figure 19-2 illustrates how container views provide the foundation of hierarchical structures:

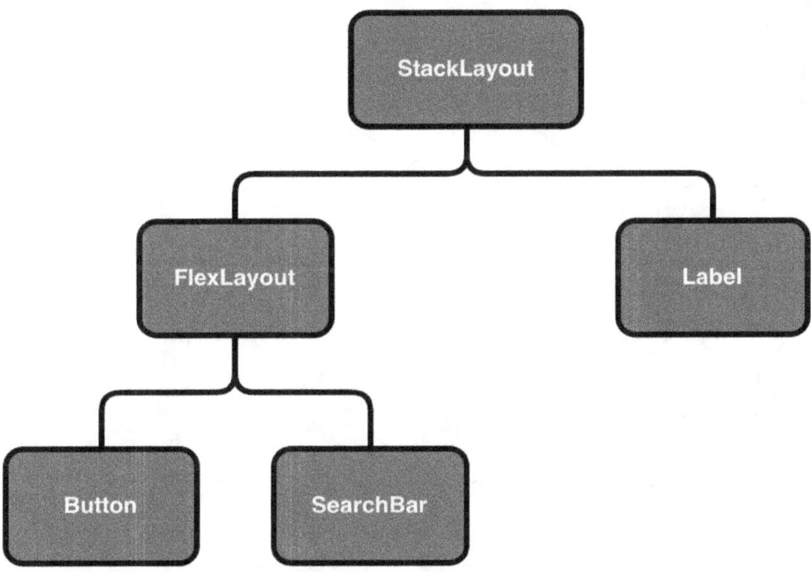


Figure 11-1

In addition to the views provided by .NET MAUI, you will also create custom views when developing apps. These custom views can contain groups of other views, with customizations to their appearance and behavior to meet the app UI requirements. The topic of custom views will be covered beginning with the chapter titled *"Building Reusable Composite Components"*.

.NET MAUI provides four layout container views that organize child views according to specific rules. StackLayout arranges elements vertically or horizontally, Grid divides the screen into rows and columns, FlexLayout adapts dynamically to available space, and AbsoluteLayout provides precise control using coordinates and proportions. By mastering these layouts, you will be able to build any interface using C# Markup.

## 11.2 Creating the LayoutDemo Project

Before we begin exploring the .NET MAUI layout views, launch Visual Studio and create a new project using our MAUIMarkup template. Name the project LayoutDemo and choose a suitable file system location before clicking the Create button.

## 11.3 StackLayout

StackLayout is the most straightforward and commonly used layout. It stacks its child elements vertically (the default) or horizontally and is ideal for forms, menus, or small sets of controls that flow in a single direction. While we can declare stack-based layouts using the StackLayout class, a more efficient approach is to use the VerticalStackLayout and HorizontalStackLayout classes.

Edit the *MainPage.cs* file as outlined below to create a simple vertical stack:

```csharp
public MainPage()
{

    Content = new VerticalStackLayout
    {
        Padding = 20,
        Spacing = 10,
        Children =
        {
            new Button
            {
                Text = "Test Button 1",
                FontSize = 18,
                HorizontalOptions = LayoutOptions.Center
            },
            new Button
            {
                Text = "Test Button 2",
                FontSize = 18,
                HorizontalOptions = LayoutOptions.Center
            },
            new Button
            {
                Text = "Test Button 3",
                FontSize = 18,
                HorizontalOptions = LayoutOptions.Center
            }
```

```
        }
    };
}
```

In the example above, the Spacing property controls the distance between views, the Padding property adds internal margins around the layout's edges, and the Children property assigns the views to be managed by the layout. Each button view is also configured to appear horizontally centered in the stack layout using values from the LayoutOptions enumeration. When the app runs, the buttons will appear as illustrated in the figure below:

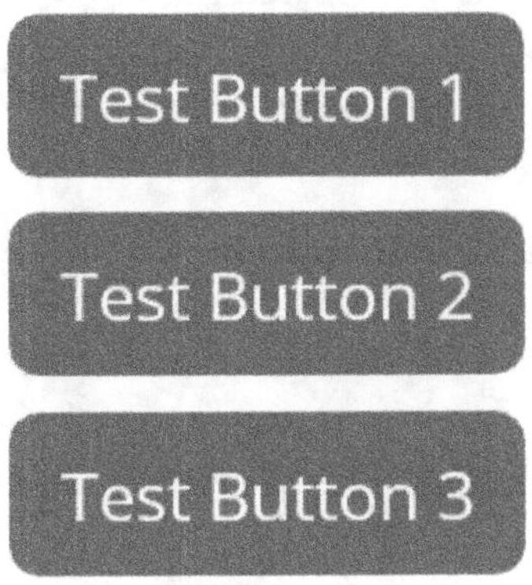


Figure 11-2

Other alignment options include Start, End, and Fill, for example:

```
new Button
{
    Text = "Test Button 1",
    FontSize = 18,
    HorizontalOptions = LayoutOptions.Start
},
new Button
{
    Text = "Test Button 2",
    FontSize = 18,
    HorizontalOptions = LayoutOptions.Fill
},
new Button
{
    Text = "Test Button 3",
    FontSize = 18,
    HorizontalOptions = LayoutOptions.End
}
```

The above changes will be rendered as shown in Figure 11-3 below:

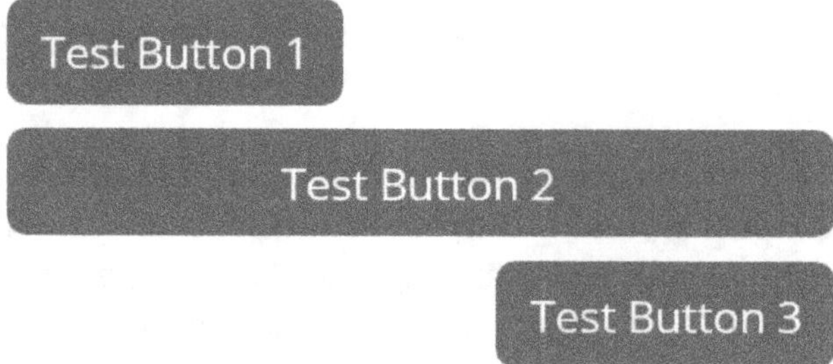


Figure 11-3

To try out the HorizontalStackLayout view, modify the example as follows:

```
public MainPage()
{
    Content = new HorizontalStackLayout
    {
        Padding = 20,
        Spacing = 10,
        Children =
        {
            new Button
            {
                Text = "Test Button 1",
                FontSize = 18,
                VerticalOptions = LayoutOptions.Start
            },
            new Button
            {
                Text = "Test Button 2",
                FontSize = 18,
                VerticalOptions = LayoutOptions.Fill
            },
            new Button
            {
                Text = "Test Button 3",
                FontSize = 18,
                VerticalOptions = LayoutOptions.End
            }
        }
    };
}
```

When the app runs, the button positioning will resemble Figure 11-4:

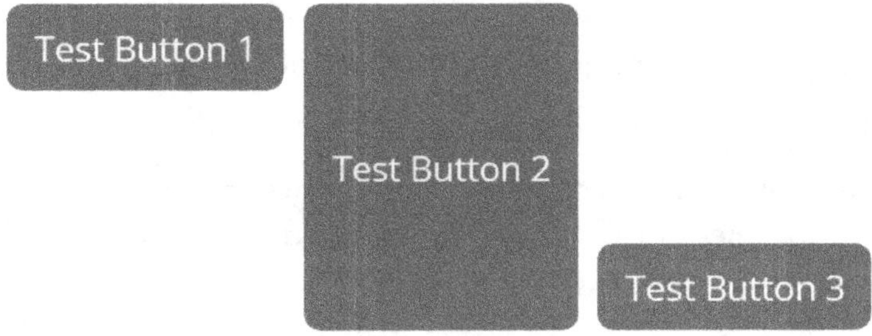


Figure 11-4

## 11.4 Dynamic Child Creation

The above examples added children to stack layouts by assigning individual view declarations to the stack view's Children property. While this works well for static layouts, we need to take a different approach when adding views dynamically.

In .NET MAUI, layout views maintain an internal list of child views using a C# IList collection, accessible through the layout instance's Children property. We can use dot notation to access this list and call methods such as Add() and Remove() to add and remove child views dynamically. In practice, this requires restructuring the code slightly so that the layout is created separately from the code that creates the children.

The following example demonstrates this approach by storing a reference to the VerticalStackLayout instance in a variable, then using a loop to add 10 Button views to the layout's child list. Finally, the updated layout is assigned to the Content property of the MainPage:

```
public MainPage()
{
    var layout = new VerticalStackLayout
    {
        Padding = 20,
        Spacing = 10
    };

    for (int i = 1; i <= 10; i++)
    {
        layout.Children.Add(new Button
        {
            Text = $"Test Button {i}",
            FontSize = 18,
            HorizontalOptions = LayoutOptions.Center
        });
    }

    Content = layout;
```

```
}
```

As a result of these changes, the user interface will consist of a vertical stack containing 10 buttons.

## 11.5 Grid Layout

The .NET MAUI Grid layout arranges content views in rows and columns by defining a matrix in which each child view occupies one or more cells specified by its row and column indices, rather like a spreadsheet.

Before we experiment with the Grid layout, we will add a new page to our project. Select the *MainPage.cs* file in the Solution Explorer, then press Ctrl-C followed by Ctrl-V to copy and paste the file. Locate the new file, which will be named *"MainPage - Copy.xaml.cs"*, rename it to *GridPage.cs*, and modify it so that it reads as follows:

```
using CommunityToolkit.Maui.Markup;


namespace LayoutDemo
{
    public partial class GridPage : ContentPage
    {
        public GridPage()
        {


        }
    }
}
```

Next, edit the *AppShell.xaml* file to add the new page and change the title of the MainPage:

```
<?xml version="1.0" encoding="UTF-8" ?>
<Shell
    x:Class="LayoutDemo.AppShell"
    xmlns="http://schemas.microsoft.com/dotnet/2021/maui"
    xmlns:x="http://schemas.microsoft.com/winfx/2009/xaml"
    xmlns:local="clr-namespace:LayoutDemo"
    Title="LayoutDemo">

    <ShellContent
        Title="Stack Layout"
        ContentTemplate="{DataTemplate local:MainPage}"
        Route="MainPage" />

    <ShellContent
        Title= "Grid Layout"
        ContentTemplate="{DataTemplate local:GridPage}"
        Route= "GridPage"/>
```

```
</Shell>
```

The Grid layout is best described by starting with an example. Returning to the *GridPage.cs* file, add the following content declaration to the GridPage() method:

```
public GridPage()
{
    Content = new Grid
    {
        Padding = 20,
        RowSpacing = 10,
        ColumnSpacing = 10,
        RowDefinitions =
        {
            new RowDefinition(GridLength.Auto),
            new RowDefinition(GridLength.Auto),
            new RowDefinition(GridLength.Auto)
        },
        ColumnDefinitions =
        {
            new ColumnDefinition(GridLength.Auto),
            new ColumnDefinition(GridLength.Auto),
            new ColumnDefinition(GridLength.Auto)
        },
        Children =
        {
            new Button { Text = "Button 1" }
                .Row(0)
                .Column(0),
            new Button { Text = "Button 2" }
                .Row(0)
                .Column(1),
            new Button { Text = "Button 3" }
                .Row(0)
                .Column(3)
                .RowSpan(2),
            new Button { Text = "Button 4" }
                .Row(1)
                .Column(0)
                .ColumnSpan(2)
        }
    };
}
```

Working with Layouts

Run the app and use the menu button indicated in Figure 11-5 to navigate to the Grid page:

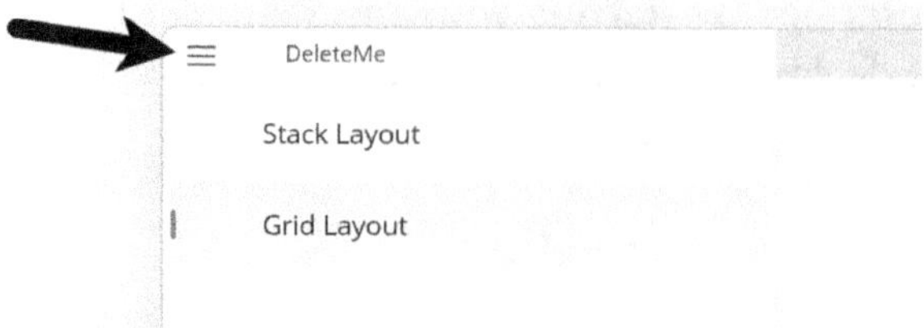


Figure 11-5

The code we have added to the GridPage() method creates a Grid containing two rows and three columns, and will appear as shown in Figure 11-6:

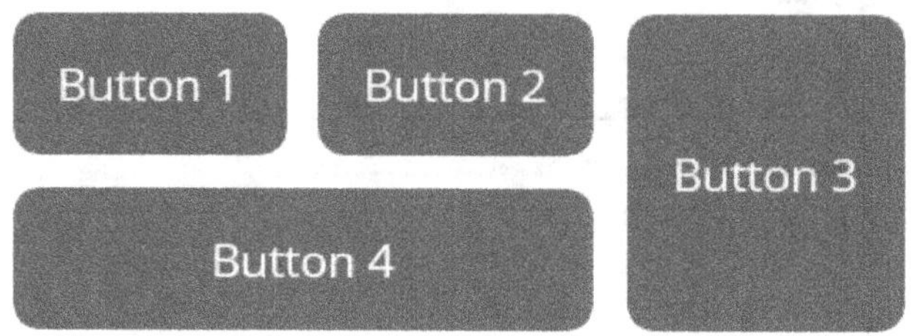


Figure 11-6

The code requires some explanation before we introduce more Grid layout features. The example begins by declaring padding around the Grid and applying spacing between the rows and columns:

```
Padding = 20,
RowSpacing = 10,
ColumnSpacing = 10,
```

Next, we define the Row and Column definitions to tell the Grid layout how each row and column should be sized:

```
RowDefinitions =
{
    new RowDefinition(GridLength.Auto),
    new RowDefinition(GridLength.Auto),
    new RowDefinition(GridLength.Auto)
},
ColumnDefinitions =
{
    new ColumnDefinition(GridLength.Auto),
    new ColumnDefinition(GridLength.Auto),
    new ColumnDefinition(GridLength.Auto)
},
```

Without these row and column definitions, the child views will be layered on top of each other, leaving only the last view visible. The size of rows and columns in a Grid is determined by a GridLength value, for which three options are available:

- **Absolute** - A fixed size in device-independent units (dp).

- **Auto** - The column or row is sized to accommodate its content.

- **Star (*)** - Takes up a proportional amount of the remaining space. For example, a column with a 2* width will be twice as wide as one with a 1* width.

The grid position of each child view is specified using the Row() and Column() extension methods. These methods may be used in conjunction with the RowSpan() and ColumnSpan() methods to spread a view across multiple cells, as we have done with buttons 3 and 4 in our example layout:

```
new Button { Text = "Button 3" }
    .Row(0)
    .Column(3)
    .RowSpan(2),
new Button { Text = "Button 4" }
    .Row(1)
    .Column(0)
    .ColumnSpan(2)
```

To demonstrate proportional sizing, adjust the column definitions as follows to replace the Auto sizing option:

```
ColumnDefinitions =
{
    new ColumnDefinition(GridLength.Star),
    new ColumnDefinition(new GridLength(2, GridUnitType.Star)),
    new ColumnDefinition(new GridLength(3, GridUnitType.Star))
},
```

These changes divide the grid width into six equal sections, allocating 1/6 of the total space to column 0, 2/6 to column 1, and the remaining half (3/6) to column 2. When the app restarts, the Grid layout will appear as shown below:

Figure 11-7

## 11.6 FlexLayout

While the Stack and Grid layouts organize content in predictable, structured ways, FlexLayout is designed for dynamic, adaptive interfaces. It is particularly useful when screen sizes and orientations differ dramatically, especially when building cross-platform apps that target phones, tablets, and desktops.

FlexLayout provides control over direction, wrapping, justification, and alignment, making it one of the most powerful containers for responsive UI design in .NET MAUI.

FlexLayout organizes its children along a main axis and a cross axis. The main axis runs in the direction specified by the Direction property, while the cross axis runs perpendicular to it. In other words, if Direction is set to Row, items flow horizontally (left to right), and if it is set to Column, items flow vertically (top to bottom).

By default, FlexLayout tries to fit all of its children into a single row or column, even if they don't all fit on the screen. The Wrap property changes this behavior. When wrapping is enabled, FlexLayout automatically starts a new "line" of items once the previous line reaches the container's width (for Row direction) or height (for Column direction).

The JustifyContent property determines how child elements are distributed along the main axis. It defines how the space between or around items is handled when there is extra room. Available options include:

- **FlexJustify.Start** – Packs children at the start of the main axis (default).

- **FlexJustify.Center** – Centers all children along the main axis.

- **FlexJustify.End** – Packs children at the end of the main axis.

- **FlexJustify.SpaceBetween** – Places equal space between children, but none at the edges.

- **FlexJustify.SpaceAround** – Places equal space around children, including edges.

- **FlexJustify.SpaceEvenly** – Distributes all items with equal space before, between, and after each child.

While JustifyContent manages distribution along the main axis, the AlignItems property controls how items align along the cross axis, which is perpendicular to the layout's direction.

Available options include:

- **FlexAlignItems.Start** –Aligns all children to the start of the cross axis.

- **FlexAlignItems.Center** – Centers all children along the cross axis.

- **FlexAlignItems.End** – Aligns children to the end of the cross axis.

- **FlexAlignItems.Stretch** – Stretches children to fill the available cross-axis space (default).

Using the Solution Explorer, select the *GridPage.cs* file and then press Ctrl-C followed by Ctrl-V to duplicate it. Locate the "*GridPage - Copy.cs*" file, rename it to *FlexPage.cs,* and modify it so that it reads as follows:

```
using CommunityToolkit.Maui.Markup;

namespace LayoutDemo
{
    public partial class FlexPage : ContentPage
```

```csharp
    {
        public FlexPage()
        {


        }
    }
}
```

Next, edit the *AppShell.xaml* file to add the new page to the navigation structure:

```xml
<?xml version="1.0" encoding="UTF-8" ?>
<Shell
    x:Class="LayoutDemo.AppShell"
    xmlns="http://schemas.microsoft.com/dotnet/2021/maui"
    xmlns:x="http://schemas.microsoft.com/winfx/2009/xaml"
    xmlns:local="clr-namespace:LayoutDemo"
    Title="LayoutDemo">

    .

    .

    <ShellContent
        Title= "Flex Layout"
        ContentTemplate="{DataTemplate local:FlexPage}"
        Route= "FlexPage"/>
</Shell>
```

To demonstrate FlexLayout's features, we will dynamically create 30 BoxView children with random colors and sizes. Return to the *FlexPage.cs* file and add the following methods to generate random color and size values:

```csharp
using CommunityToolkit.Maui.Markup;
using Microsoft.Maui.Layouts;


namespace LayoutDemo
{
    public partial class FlexPage : ContentPage
    {
        private static readonly Random random = new();

        public FlexPage()
        {


        }


        private static int GetRandomNumber(int min, int max)
        {
```

```
            return random.Next(min, max);
    }


    private static Color GetRandomColor()
    {
        float r = (float)random.NextDouble();
        float g = (float)random.NextDouble();
        float b = (float)random.NextDouble();


        return Color.FromRgb(r, g, b);
    }

    }
}
```

The next steps involve creating a FlexLayout instance and constructing a loop that adds the BoxView children configured with random color and width properties:

```
using CommunityToolkit.Maui.Markup;
using Microsoft.Maui.Layouts;

namespace LayoutDemo
{
    public partial class FlexPage : ContentPage
    {
        private static readonly Random random = new();

        public FlexPage()
        {
            var layout = new FlexLayout
            {
                Padding = 10,
                Direction = FlexDirection.Row,
                Wrap = FlexWrap.Wrap,
                JustifyContent = FlexJustify.Start,
                AlignItems = FlexAlignItems.End
            };

            for (int i = 1; i < 30; i++)
            {
                int randomDimension = GetRandomNumber(50, 100);

                layout.Children.Add(
                    new BoxView
```

```
        {
            Color = GetRandomColor()
        }
        .Size(randomDimension, 60)
    );
}

.
.

    Content = layout;
}
```

The FlexLayout instance above is configured to arrange its children horizontally along the main axis and to wrap to the next row when space is limited. We have also specified that the children are to be justified on the left edge of the main axis and aligned on the bottom edge of the cross axis.

Run the app and resize the window to constrain the available space, forcing the layout to occupy multiple rows, as shown in Figure 11-8 below:

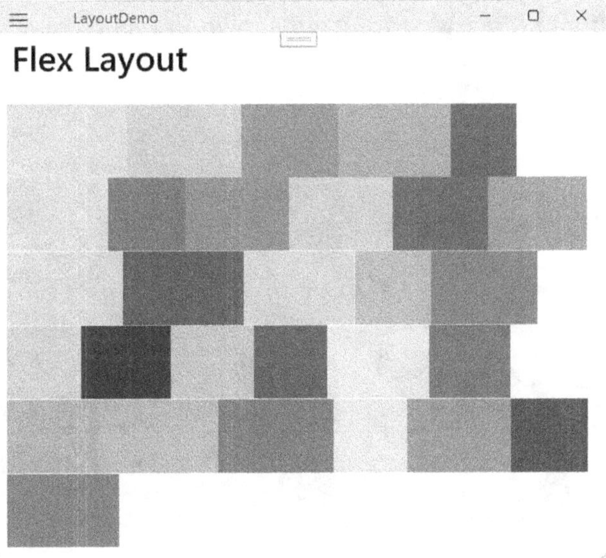


Figure 11-8

Note that, unlike the Grid layout, the child views are not constrained by cell boundaries or proportions, and appear in their intended sizes.

Make the following modifications to the layout to demonstrate the cross axis alignment and spacing properties:

```
var layout = new FlexLayout
{
    Padding = 10,
    Direction = FlexDirection.Row,
```

```
    Wrap = FlexWrap.Wrap,
    JustifyContent = FlexJustify.SpaceBetween,
    AlignItems = FlexAlignItems.End
};


for (int i = 1; i < 30; i++)
{
    int randomDimension = GetRandomNumber(50, 100);

    layout.Children.Add(
        new BoxView
        {
            Color = GetRandomColor()
        }
        .Size(randomDimension, randomDimension)
    );
}
```

When the app runs, it should resemble the layout shown in Figure 11-9:

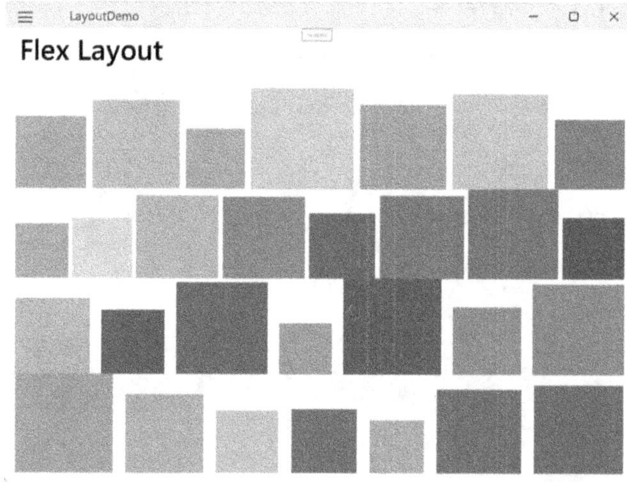


Figure 11-9

## 11.7 AbsoluteLayout

AbsoluteLayout positions its children using explicit x and y coordinates and proportional positioning. Begin by creating a new page named AbsolutePage using the previous steps, and add it to the *AppShell.xaml* structure so that it is accessible from the navigation menu. Edit the *AbsolutePage.cs* file and declare an AbsoluteLayout containing a single BoxView child:

```
using CommunityToolkit.Maui.Markup;
using Microsoft.Maui.Layouts;
```

```
namespace LayoutDemo
{
    public partial class AbsolutePage : ContentPage
    {
        public AbsolutePage()
        {
            Content = new AbsoluteLayout
            {
                Children =
                {
                    new BoxView { Color = Colors.DarkBlue }
                }
            }
            .BackgroundColor(Colors.Silver);
        }
    }
}
```

The size and position of individual AbsoluteLayout children are controlled using the LayoutBounds() and LayoutFlags() extension methods. The LayoutBounds() method specifies the x and y coordinates (where 0, 0 represents the top-left corner of the parent), as well as the height and width, of the corresponding view. The following code change, for example, draws the box centered at pixel position 50, 80, sized 100 pixels wide and 200 pixels high:

```
new BoxView { Color = Colors.DarkBlue }
    .LayoutBounds(50, 80, 100, 200)
```

By default, the AbsoluteLayout parent interprets the bounds settings as absolute. In other words, the values are treated as pixels that define the precise position and size of the view. This behavior can be changed by calling the LayoutFlags() method and passing it one of the following values from the AbsoluteLayoutFlags enumeration:

- **None** – All values are treated as absolute.

- **XProportional** – The x coordinate is interpreted as proportional. The other values are absolute.

- **YProportional** - The y coordinate is interpreted as proportional. The other values are absolute.

- **WidthProportional** - The width is interpreted as proportional. All other values are absolute.

- **HeightProportional** - The height is interpreted as proportional. All other values are absolute.

- **PositionProportional** - The x and y coordinates are interpreted as proportional. Size values are treated as absolute.

- **SizeProportional** - The width and height values are interpreted as proportional. Position values are absolute.

Working with Layouts

- **All** - All coordinate and size values are interpreted as proportional.

Proportional values are declared as percentages represented by values between 0 and 1. To see this in action, modify the BoxView declaration to use proportional values:

```
Content = new AbsoluteLayout
{
    Children =
    {
        new BoxView { Color = Colors.DarkBlue }
            .LayoutFlags(AbsoluteLayoutFlags.All)
            .LayoutBounds(0.5, 0.5, 0.65, 0.65)
    }
}
.BackgroundColor(Colors.Silver);
```

The above changes position the box in the center of the parent layout, sized at 65% of the parent's height and width. The key point here is that these proportions are maintained even when the parent's dimensions change, allowing us to design responsive layouts that adapt to changes in window and screen size, as well as device orientation. Run the app and verify that the proportions are maintained irrespective of the window size:

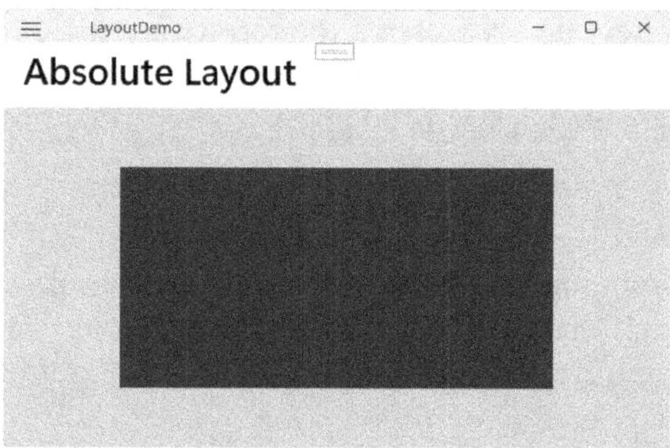


Figure 11-10

## 11.8 Summary

Layouts form the structural framework of a .NET MAUI application, determining how visual elements are organized and rendered. The StackLayout provides a simple, sequential arrangement of controls, while the Grid enables precise, two-dimensional placement through defined rows and columns. FlexLayout provides adaptive behavior for responsive interfaces, while AbsoluteLayout enables precise positioning when pixel-level control is necessary.

In the next chapter, you will build upon this foundation by learning how to work with controls and input elements in C# Markup, exploring how they interact with layouts, and how to handle user input cleanly.

# 12. Views, Controls, and Event Handling

Now that we understand how layouts provide the structure of user interface designs, it's time to explore the individual building blocks that make up those layouts: views and controls.

In this chapter, you will learn how to create and configure common controls using C# Markup, apply properties fluently, and handle user input and commands entirely in code.

## 12.1 Understanding Views in .NET MAUI

Views provide the basis for .NET MAUI UI design and are responsible for rendering content on the screen and handling user interaction.

They are broadly categorized as either *display views* or *interactive views*. Display views, such as Label, Image, and BoxView, present content to the user, while interactive controls, including Button, Entry, Switch, and Slider, enable users to input data or trigger events.

All of these derive from the View base class and can be placed inside layouts (which are also views) to form a page hierarchy.

When using C# Markup, you create and configure each view in code by chaining fluent methods to set properties, rather than assigning them in XAML. This not only makes the code concise but also allows for reuse and composition.

## 12.2 The Label Control

The Label control displays text and is one of the simplest yet most frequently used elements in any .NET MAUI app. In C# Markup, a label can be created and styled with fluent syntax, as shown below:

```
new Label()
    .Text("Welcome to C# Markup")
    .Font(size: 36)
    .CenterHorizontal();
```

Here, the Text() method sets the label's content, Font() adjusts the text size, and CenterHorizontal() aligns the label within its parent layout. Using these fluent methods makes configuration readable and intuitive.

You can also create multiline labels and set text wrapping or truncation via the LineBreakMode property:

```
new Label
```

```
{
    Text = "This is a long line of text that will wrap automatically when
it reaches the edge of the screen.",
    LineBreakMode = LineBreakMode.WordWrap,
    WidthRequest = 300
};
```

## 12.3 The Button Control

The Button view is an interactive control that can be created and styled using the same fluent syntax, and to which we can attach event handlers to perform tasks in response to clicks. For example:

```
new Button()
    .Text("Click Me")
    .Font(size: 18)
    .BackgroundColor(Colors.CadetBlue)
    .TextColor(Colors.White)
    .Invoke(b => b.Clicked += OnButtonClicked);
```

The Invoke() method lets us attach an event handler inline, making it easy to wire up logic. The corresponding event handler method for the above button declaration might read as follows:

```
void OnButtonClicked(object? sender, EventArgs e)
{
    if (sender is Button button)
    {
        button.Text = "Clicked!";
    }
}
```

## 12.4 Understanding the Invoke() Method

In C# Markup, the Invoke() method serves as a bridge between declarative UI construction and event handling, allowing us to execute an inline action on the control being created. This allows you to attach event handlers or perform additional configuration inline, without breaking the flow of chained method calls.

Consider our previous example:

```
new Button()
    .Text("Click Me")
    .Font(size: 18)
    .BackgroundColor(Colors.CadetBlue)
    .TextColor(Colors.White)
    .Invoke(b => b.Clicked += OnButtonClicked);
```

Here, the Invoke() method receives a lambda expression that takes the button instance (b) as its argument. Within the lambda, we can access any of the button control's members, such as its properties or events. In C# terminology, the OnButtonClicked event handler is said to be subscribed to the button's Click event.

Without Invoke(), we would have to assign the event handler after constructing the button, which would disrupt the declarative flow of the fluent syntax. For example:

```
var button = new Button()
    .Text("Click Me")
    .Font(size: 18)
    .BackgroundColor(Colors.CadetBlue)
    .TextColor(Colors.White)


button.Clicked += OnButtonClicked;
```

While functionally identical, this approach separates object creation and event configuration. The fluent version keeps everything in line, improving readability while maintaining the declarative structure.

Note that we subscribe the event handler to the click event using the += operator instead of the regular assignment operator (=). Interactive controls, such as the button, maintain an internal list of subscribed event handlers to be invoked when the event is triggered. By using the += operator, we append the OnButtonClicked method to any other event handlers that may have already been subscribed. We can, for example, configure our button to call two methods when clicked:

```
var button = new Button()
    .Text("Click Me")
    .Font(size: 18)
    .BackgroundColor(Colors.CadetBlue)
    .TextColor(Colors.White);


button.Clicked += ClickHandlerOne;
button.Clicked += ClickHandlerTwo;
```

Conversely, we can remove event handlers from the control's invocation list using the -= operator as follows:

```
button.Clicked -= ClickHandlerTwo;
```

## 12.5 The Entry Control

The Entry control is frequently used in forms and login screens, providing a single-line text input field for user input. The following code shows a typical Entry declaration:

```
new Entry()
    .Placeholder("Enter your name")
    .TextColor(Colors.DarkSlateGray)
    .Font(size: 18)
    .Margin(10)
    .Invoke(e => e.TextChanged += OnTextChanged);
```

```
void OnTextChanged(object? sender, TextChangedEventArgs e)
{
    System.Diagnostics.Debug.WriteLine($"Old: {e.OldTextValue}, " +
                        $"New: {e.NewTextValue}");
}
```

In addition to the control instance that triggered the event, the subscribed event handler methods are also sent an event argument instance specific to the control type. In the above example, the Entry control passes a TextChangedEventArgs object to the event handler from which we can extract the before and after text for each keystroke.

## 12.6 The Image Control

Images are used for branding, decoration, or visual communication. In .NET MAUI, images can be loaded from embedded resources, local files, or remote URLs.

The following declaration initializes an Image control with a built-in .NET MAUI image:

```
new Image()
    .Source("dotnet_bot.png")
    .Aspect(Aspect.AspectFit)
    .CenterHorizontal();
```

The Aspect property determines how the image scales within its bounds and provides the following options:

- **AspectFit** – Fits the image within the view.

- **AspectFill** – Fills the view, cropping parts.

- **Fill** – Stretches the image to fill all space.

## 12.7 Other Common Controls

Other controls include Switch, Slider, Stepper, ProgressBar, and DatePicker. Each follows the same fluent pattern for configuration, for example:

```
new Slider
{
    Minimum = 0,
    Maximum = 100,
    Value = 25
}
.Invoke(s => s.ValueChanged += OnSliderChanged);

void OnSliderChanged(object? sender, ValueChangedEventArgs e)
{
    if (sender is Slider slider)
```

```
    {
        System.Diagnostics.Debug.WriteLine(
            $"Slider value changed to {slider.Value}");
    }
}
```

## 12.8 Binding Commands and Handling Events

Event handling is straightforward using Invoke(), but command binding offers a cleaner approach when following the MVVM pattern, a topic we will cover in the *"MVVM and Data Binding in C# Markup"* chapter.

## 12.9 Summary

Views and controls are the building blocks of user interface design in .NET MAUI, providing users with information and interactivity.

Labels present information, while buttons and entry fields collect user input, and images enhance the visual experience. The fluent methods make configuration straightforward, and commands and events seamlessly connect your user interface to the underlying logic.

# 13. MVVM and Data Binding in C# Markup

Data binding is one of the most important mechanisms in .NET MAUI and is essential for keeping the user interface and application data synchronized. It does this by providing a declarative way to connect properties of UI elements to data or commands in the underlying model, ensuring that changes to one are automatically reflected in the other. When the data in a ViewModel changes, the UI updates automatically. Conversely, when the user interacts with the UI, the underlying data can be updated accordingly.

When combined with C# Markup and the CommunityToolkit.Mvvm library, data binding allows us to express bindings fluently in code without relying on XAML.

## 13.1 The MVVM Pattern in .NET MAUI

The Model-View-ViewModel (MVVM) pattern organizes an application into three distinct parts:

- **Model** – The underlying data or business logic.

- **View** – The visual interface presented to the user.

- **ViewModel** – The mediator that exposes the data and commands the View binds to.

The ViewModel holds observable state and encapsulates app logic while the View defines only presentation, using bindings to link its properties to the ViewModel's data. This structure achieves clear separation of concerns: the UI layer can evolve independently of the data model, and logic can be tested without requiring the full UI to run.

Data binding is the mechanism that connects these layers. In C# Markup, bindings are declared fluently using the Bind() extension method rather than in XAML, producing fully declarative bindings in code.

## 13.2 Using ObservableObject and [ObservableProperty]

In traditional MVVM, developers manually implement INotifyPropertyChanged to signal when a property changes. While functional, this approach required extra code, resulting in code that was hard to read and understand. The CommunityToolkit.Mvvm package simplifies this with three key features: the ObservableObject base class and the [ObservableProperty] and [RelayCommand] attributes.

The ObservableObject base class already implements INotifyPropertyChanged, including helper methods such as SetProperty() and OnPropertyChanged(). ViewModels that inherit from ObservableObject automatically gain the ability to raise change notifications whenever a property's value is updated.

The [ObservableProperty] attribute takes this a step further. When applied to a field in a partial class, it instructs the source generator to automatically create a public property and handle all of the notification logic. This generated property includes a private backing field.

A private backing field is an internal variable that "backs" a property — meaning it stores the value the property represents. In standard C#, you might write:

```csharp
private string name;
public string Name
{
    get => name;
    set
    {
        if (name != value)
        {
            name = value;
            OnPropertyChanged(nameof(Name));
        }
    }
}
```

In the above example, *name* is the private backing field for the public *Name* property. It keeps the data encapsulated while allowing the property to expose it safely through getter and setter accessors. This separation ensures that you can perform logic (such as validation or notifications) inside the setter without directly exposing the internal field. When using [ObservableProperty], this backing field and the associated property code are generated automatically by the build system. For example:

```csharp
[ObservableProperty]
public partial string Name { get; set; }
```

The source generator produces equivalent code to the manual version above — including the private field, the public property, and the logic to raise PropertyChanged when the value changes. This drastically reduces boilerplate while maintaining the same behavior and encapsulation principles:

```csharp
using CommunityToolkit.Mvvm.ComponentModel;
using CommunityToolkit.Mvvm.Input;


public partial class MainViewModel : ObservableObject
{
    [ObservableProperty]
    public partial string Name { get; set; }

    [ObservableProperty]
```

```csharp
    public partial string Message { get; set; }

    [RelayCommand]
    void Submit()
    {
        Message = $"Welcome, {Name}!";
    }
}
```

The [ObservableProperty] attributes generate Name and Message properties, each with its own private backing field and automatic notifications. The [RelayCommand] attribute generates a corresponding command named SubmitCommand for use in bindings.

## 13.3 Understanding [RelayCommand]

In MVVM configurations, user interactions such as button clicks, toggles, and menu selections are handled through commands instead of event handlers. This approach decouples the user interface from the logic it triggers, maintaining a clean separation between View and ViewModel.

Traditionally, this required implementing the ICommand interface or instantiating a Command object manually within the ViewModel. The CommunityToolkit.Mvvm library greatly simplifies this process through the [RelayCommand] attribute.

### 13.3.1 How [RelayCommand] Works

The [RelayCommand] attribute, when applied to a method inside a class derived from ObservableObject, automatically generates an ICommand property that invokes that method. The generated property follows the naming convention of appending "Command" to the method name. For example:

```csharp
using CommunityToolkit.Mvvm.ComponentModel;
using CommunityToolkit.Mvvm.Input;

public partial class CounterViewModel : ObservableObject
{
    [ObservableProperty]
    public partial int Count { get; set; }

    [RelayCommand]
    void Increment()
    {
        Count++;
    }
}
```

At build time, the source generator creates a corresponding property named IncrementCommand, which implements the ICommand interface. You can then bind this command directly to a UI control, such as a Button, without writing any additional command-related code:

```
new Button()
    .Text("Increment")
    .Bind(Button.CommandProperty, nameof(CounterViewModel.
IncrementCommand));
```

When the user taps the button, the command automatically invokes the Increment() method in the ViewModel. Because Increment() updates the Count property (decorated with [ObservableProperty]), the UI reacts immediately through data binding.

### 13.3.2 Commands with Parameters

Commands can also accept parameters. Simply define a method with one or more parameters, and the toolkit will generate a matching command property that accepts them:

```
[RelayCommand]
void Greet(string name)
{
    Message = $"Hello, {name}!";
}
```

The example generates GreetCommand, which can be invoked and passed a name value by binding to CommandProperty and CommandParameterProperty, as shown below:

```
new Button()
    .Text("Greet")
    .Bind(Button.CommandProperty, nameof(MainViewModel.GreetCommand))
    .Bind(Button.CommandParameterProperty, "Jason")
}
```

## 13.4 Establishing the BindingContext in C# Markup

Every page or layout that requires view model access needs a BindingContext object the properties of which the UI will bind to. In C# Markup, this is set programmatically, usually within the page's constructor. Consider the following page declaration:

```
public class MainPage : ContentPage
{
    public MainPage()
    {
        var viewModel = new MainViewModel();
        BindingContext = viewModel;

        Content = new StackLayout()
            .Padding(20)
            .Spacing(15)
            .Children(
                new Label()
```

```
            .Text("Enter your name:")
            .Font(size: 18),

        new Entry()
            .Placeholder("Type here")
            .Bind(Entry.TextProperty, nameof(MainViewModel.Name),
                    mode: BindingMode.TwoWay),

        new Button()
            .Text("Submit")
            .Bind(Button.CommandProperty,
                    nameof(MainViewModel.SubmitCommand)),

        new Label()
            .Bind(Label.TextProperty,
                    nameof(MainViewModel.Message))
            .Font(size: 18)
            .TextColor(Colors.DarkSlateBlue)
        );
    }
}
```

The MainPage() method begins by creating an instance of the view model and assigning it to the BindingContext. In the content declaration, the Entry view binds to the Name property in TwoWay mode, so user input updates the ViewModel, and ViewModel changes are reflected in the UI. The Button is bound to the auto-generated SubmitCommand, and the Label shows the current Message.

## 13.5 Understanding Binding Modes

The BindingMode property determines the direction in which data flows between the View (UI) and the ViewModel (data source). The most common modes in .NET MAUI are OneWay and TwoWay.

OneWay binding means that data flows only from the ViewModel to the View. When the ViewModel property changes, the UI updates automatically; however, any user interaction with the control does not modify the property. This is ideal for displaying information that the user does not edit, such as labels or read-only indicators, for example:

```
new Label()
    .Bind(Label.TextProperty, nameof(MainViewModel.Message),
            mode: BindingMode.OneWay);
```

In the above case, the label will update whenever the ViewModel's Message property changes, but changes in the UI (if possible) will not propagate back.

TwoWay Binding, on the other hand, allows data to flow in both directions. When the ViewModel updates, the UI reflects the change, and when the user modifies the control, the new value is automatically written back to the ViewModel property.

TwoWay mode is typically used for input elements, such as Entry, Editor, CheckBox, or Switch:

```
new Entry()
    .Bind(Entry.TextProperty, nameof(MainViewModel.Name),
            mode: BindingMode.TwoWay);
```

Text typed into the entry field updates the Name property, and any code changes to Name within the view model are immediately reflected in the entry's text.

The distinction is vital for performance and clarity. OneWay is sufficient for static displays, while TwoWay provides full interactivity when you need to capture user input.

The default mode in the absence of a specific settings depends on the property type. By default, a property type that can be read and written to, such as an Entry view's text property, will default to TwoWay mode, while the read-only property of a Label view will default to OneWay. Bindings to command parameters on the other hand, always default to OneWay.

Although less common in C# Markup, .NET MAUI also supports the following binding modes:

- **OneTime** – Data is transferred from source to target only once when the binding is initialized.

- **OneWayToSource** – Data flows only from the View to the ViewModel.

## 13.6 Declarative Bindings and Reactive Updates

Bindings can connect any bindable property of a control to any observable property in the ViewModel. The Bind() extension method in C# Markup mirrors what XAML bindings do, but with full compile-time support.

Binding a label's text:

```
new Label()
    .Bind(Label.TextProperty, nameof(MainViewModel.Message));
```

TwoWay binding for inputs:

```
new Entry()
    .Bind(Entry.TextProperty, nameof(MainViewModel.Name),
            mode: BindingMode.TwoWay);
```

Because ObservableObject raises PropertyChanged automatically, every property decorated with [ObservableProperty] participates in this reactive update system. There's no need to call OnPropertyChanged() or define backing fields manually—everything is generated for us at build time.

## 13.7 Summary

This chapter introduced the data binding mechanisms that implement the Model–View–ViewModel (MVVM) architecture in .NET MAUI, demonstrating how to use these concepts with C# Markup. The key role of the MVVM pattern is to maintain a clear separation between presentation logic and data management while ensuring that the user interface and underlying data are synchronized. We also learned about the CommunityToolkit.Mvvm library and explored how the ObservableObject base class and the [ObservableProperty] attribute simplify the implementation of property change notifications. We also highlighted the use of [RelayCommand] to automatically generate command bindings, thereby connecting user interface interaction with the ViewModel logic code.

# 14. An MVVM Data Binding Tutorial

Now that we understand MVVM and data binding in .NET MAUI, we are ready to put theory into practice by creating an example project. The project will provide a demonstration of MVVM patterns, observable objects and properties, data binding, and command relays.

## 14.1 Creating the BindingDemo Project

Start Visual Studio and create a new project named MvvmDemo using the MauiMarkup project template.

## 14.2 Adding the View Model

The first requirement for our project is a view model class containing the data and logic for our app. Within Visual Studio, display the Solution Explorer, right-click on the MvvmDemo entry at the top of the solution tree, and select the *Add -> Class...* menu option. In the new item dialog, name the class *MainViewModel.cs* and click the Add button.

Once the class has been added, modify it so that it reads as follows:

```
using CommunityToolkit.Mvvm.ComponentModel;


namespace MvvmDemo
{
    public partial class MainViewModel : ObservableObject
    {


    }
}
```

## 14.3 Declaring the Observable Properties and Command

The completed app will require observable properties to store user input from an Entry view and an integer that we will bind to a Slider control. Remaining in the *MainViewModel.cs* file, add these properties as outlined below:

```
using CommunityToolkit.Mvvm.ComponentModel;


namespace MvvmDemo
{
    public partial class MainViewModel : ObservableObject
    {
        [ObservableProperty]
        public partial string Title { get; set; } = "Hello, MVVM!";
```

```
        [ObservableProperty]
            public partial int TextSize { get; set; }
    }
}
```

Finally, the view model needs a Command that can be called to reset the data properties to their default values:

```
using CommunityToolkit.Mvvm.ComponentModel;
using CommunityToolkit.Mvvm.Input;


namespace MvvmDemo
{
    public partial class MainViewModel : ObservableObject
    {
        [ObservableProperty]
            public partial string Title { get; set; } = "Hello, MVVM!";

        [ObservableProperty]
            public partial int TextSize { get; set; }

        [RelayCommand]
        void Reset()
        {
            TextSize = 18;
            Title = "";
        }
    }
}
```

At this point, the editor may report problems with the Title and TextSize properties. This is because partial properties are a new C# feature. To resolve this issue, right-click on the MvvmDemo entry in the Solution Explorer and select the "Edit Project File" menu option. When the project file appears in the code editor, make the following addition:

```
<Project Sdk="Microsoft.NET.Sdk">


    <PropertyGroup>
            <LangVersion>preview</LangVersion>
    </PropertyGroup>


    <PropertyGroup>
            <TargetFrameworks>net10.0-android</TargetFrameworks>
    .

    .
```

## 14.4 Designing the View Layout

The app's user interface will consist of Entry, Slider, Button, and Label controls, arranged in a vertical stack layout. Edit the *MainPage.cs* file and declare the following page layout:

```csharp
using CommunityToolkit.Maui.Markup;


namespace MvvmDemo
{

    public partial class MainPage : ContentPage
    {
        public MainPage()
        {
            Content = new VerticalStackLayout
            {
                Padding = 20,
                Spacing = 20,
                Children =
                {
                    new Entry
                    {
                        HorizontalOptions = LayoutOptions.Center
                    }
                    .Placeholder("Enter text here"),

                    new Slider {
                        Minimum = 18,
                        Maximum = 100,
                        Value = 50,
                        WidthRequest = 300
                    },

                    new Button()
                        .Text("Reset")
                        .Font(size: 20)
                        .CenterHorizontal(),

                    new Label()
                        .Text("Sample Text")
                        .CenterHorizontal()
                }
            };
        }
}
```

```
    }
}
```

Run the app and verify that it matches the layout in Figure 14-1 below:

Figure 14-1

## 14.5 Adding the Bindings

The final step is to add the property and command bindings. Return to the *MainPage.cs* file and make the following changes to the Entry declaration:

```csharp
public MainPage()
{
    var viewModel = new MainViewModel();
    BindingContext = viewModel;

    Content = new VerticalStackLayout
    {
        Padding = 20,
        Spacing = 20,
        Children =
        {
            new Entry
            {
                HorizontalOptions = LayoutOptions.Center
            }
            .Placeholder("Enter text here")
            .Bind(Entry.TextProperty, nameof(MainViewModel.Title)),
.
.
```

In addition to setting up the BindingContext, the above changes also bind the Entry's text property to the view model's Title property. Next, bind the Slider value to the TextSize property:

```
new Slider {
    Minimum = 18,
    Maximum = 100,
    Value = 50,
    WidthRequest = 300
}
.Bind(Slider.ValueProperty, nameof(MainViewModel.TextSize)),
```

Finally, bind the Button to the Reset command and configure the Label to display the current Title value using the TextSize property to specify the font size:

```
new Button()
    .Text("Reset")
    .Font(size: 20)
    .CenterHorizontal()
    .Bind(Button.CommandProperty, nameof(MainViewModel.ResetCommand)),

new Label()
    .Text("Sample Text")
    .CenterHorizontal()
    .Bind(Label.FontSizeProperty, nameof(MainViewModel.TextSize))
    .Bind(Label.TextProperty, nameof(MainViewModel.Title))
```

## 14.6 Testing the App

Build and run the app and experiment with entering text, adjusting the slider, and clicking the Reset button. The UI should update dynamically in response to each property change:

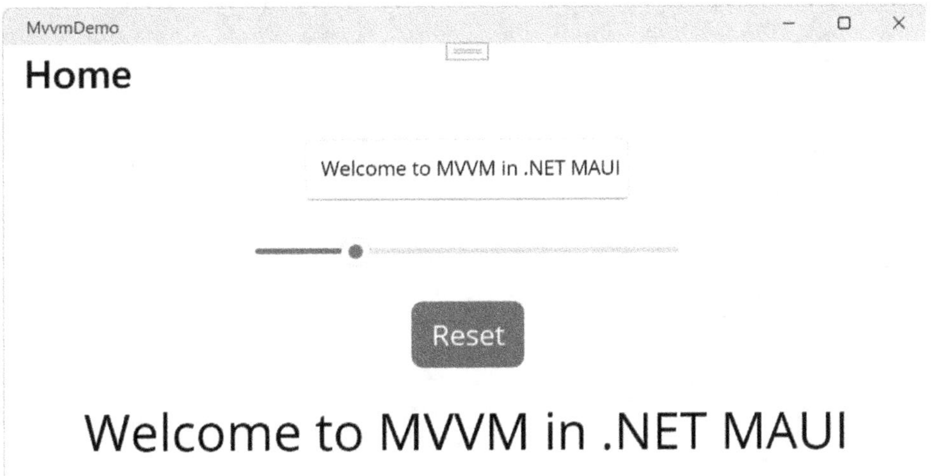


Figure 14-2

## 14.7 Summary

In this chapter, we developed an application that illustrates how to implement an MVVM (Model-View-ViewModel) structure. We used both property and relay command binding to synchronize the user interface with the underlying model data. The steps involved declaring the view model, creating observable properties and commands, and binding the user interface components to them.

# 15. Working with Styling and Fonts

This chapter explores how to control the appearance of a .NET MAUI app using styles, resources, and fonts in C# Markup. You will learn how to create reusable visual definitions, apply them to controls explicitly or implicitly, and use style inheritance to maintain visual consistency across the app.

## 15.1 Creating the StyleDemo Project

Throughout this chapter, we will use an example project to demonstrate how to use styles in C# Markup and .NET MAUI. Begin by starting Visual Studio and creating a new project named StyleDemo using the MauiMarkup template.

## 15.2 Applying Styles with Fluent Extensions

A style defines a collection of property values that can be applied repeatedly across multiple controls. Its purpose is to eliminate visual inconsistency and duplication. Instead of setting colors, fonts, or padding for every control manually, styles let you encapsulate those decisions once and reuse them.

In C# Markup, styles are represented by the Style<T> class, where T is the target control type (for example, Button, Slider,  or Label), using the following syntax:

```
var customStyle = new Style<type>()
    .Add(property1)
    .Add(property2) ...
```

To apply a style to a view, we use the Style() extension method or set the Style property as outlined below:

```
new Label()
.

.

    .Style(customStyle)


new Label
{
.

.

    Style = customStyle

}
```

Edit the *MainPage.cs* file and make the following changes to the MainPage() method to create a style and apply it to a Label control:

```csharp
public MainPage()
{
    var headerStyle = new Style<Label>()
        .Add(Label.FontSizeProperty, 32)
        .Add(Label.FontAttributesProperty, FontAttributes.Bold)
        .Add(Label.TextColorProperty, Colors.White)
        .Add(Label.BackgroundColorProperty, Colors.Crimson)
        .Add(Label.PaddingProperty, new Thickness(5));

    Content = new VerticalStackLayout
    {
        Spacing = 20,
        Padding = 20,
        Children = {
            new Label()
                .Text("A Label with Style")
                .CenterHorizontal()
                .Style(headerStyle)
        }
    };
}
```

When the app runs, the label should appear as illustrated in Figure 15-1:

Figure 15-1

Although we specified the Label type for the style, it can also be applied to other types that share the same properties. Our headerStyle, for example, can be applied to a Button because the properties it contains are common to both types. Experiment by adding a Button control to the MainPage layout and applying the headerStyle to it:

```csharp
public MainPage()
{
    .

    .

    Content = new VerticalStackLayout
    {
        Spacing = 20,
        Padding = 20,
        Children = {
            new Label()
```

```
        .Text("A Label with Style")
        .CenterHorizontal()
        .Style(headerStyle),

    new Button()
        .Text("A Button to Click")
        .CenterHorizontal()
        .Style(headerStyle)
    }
  };
}
```

Run the app and note that the style has been applied to both controls:

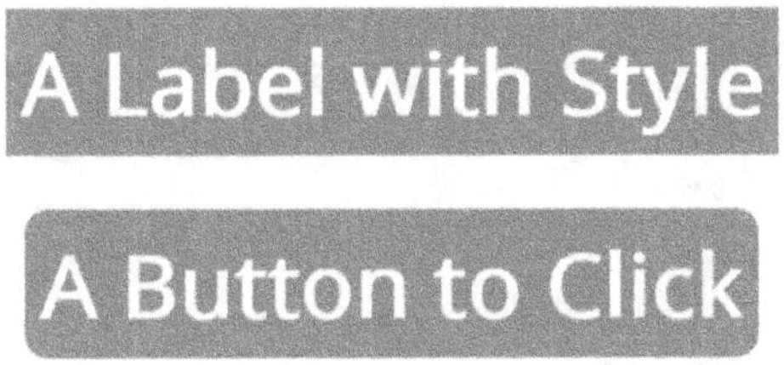

Figure 15-2

Although this example works, the same would not be true if headerStyle contained a property that is not shared by the Button and Label controls, such as MaxLinesProperty:

```
var headerStyle = new Style<Label>()
    .Add(Label.FontSizeProperty, 32)
    .Add(Label.FontAttributesProperty, FontAttributes.Bold)
    .Add(Label.TextColorProperty, Colors.White)
    .Add(Label.BackgroundColorProperty, Colors.Crimson)
    .Add(Label.PaddingProperty, new Thickness(5))
    .Add(Label.MaxLinesProperty, 10);
```

Attempting to apply headerStyle to the Button control after this change will trigger the following runtime exception:

```
System.InvalidCastException: 'Unable to cast object of type 'Microsoft.
Maui.Controls.Button' to type 'Microsoft.Maui.Controls.Label'.'
```

For this reason, it is best to avoid mixing styles and types unless you know exactly what you are doing. Before proceeding, modify the MainPage() method as follows in preparation for the next section:

```
public MainPage()
{
    var headerStyle = new Style<Label>()
        .Add(Label.FontSizeProperty, 32)
```

```
            .Add(Label.MaxLinesProperty, 10);

    Content = new VerticalStackLayout
    {
        Spacing = 20,
        Padding = 20,
        Children = {



            new Button()
                .Text("A Button to Click")
                .CenterHorizontal()
                .Style(headerStyle)
        }
    };
}
```

## 15.3 Explicit and Implicit Styles

The headerStyle declaration above is an example of an *explicit style*. Explicit styles must be applied manually to individual controls and are ideal when different controls require distinct appearances. *Implicit styles*, on the other hand, are automatically applied to every control of the specified type within the context of the entire app or current page.

Implicit styles are defined as ResourceDictionary instances using similar syntax to explicit styles, and a single ResourceDictionary object can contain multiple styles:

```
Resources = new ResourceDictionary
{
    new Style<type>()
        .Add(property1)
        .Add(property2),
    new Style<type>()
        .Add(property3)



    };
```

## 15.4 An Implicit Style Example

To experience implicit styles, begin by duplicating the *MainPage.cs*, file by selecting it in the Solution Explorer and pressing Ctrl-C followed by Ctrl-V to copy and paste the file. Locate the new file, which will be named "*MainPage - Copy.xaml.cs*", rename it to *SecondPage.cs*, and modify it so that it reads as follows:

```csharp
using CommunityToolkit.Maui.Markup;

namespace StyleDemo
{
    public partial class SecondPage : ContentPage
    {
        public SecondPage()
        {
            var headerStyle = new Style<Label>()
                .Add(Label.FontSizeProperty, 32)
                .Add(Label.FontAttributesProperty, FontAttributes.Bold)
                .Add(Label.TextColorProperty, Colors.White)
                .Add(Label.BackgroundColorProperty, Colors.Crimson)
                .Add(Label.PaddingProperty, new Thickness(5));

            Content = new VerticalStackLayout
            {
                Spacing = 20,
                Padding = 20,
                Children =
                {
                    new Label()
                        .Text("A Label with Implicit Style")
                        .CenterHorizontal(),

                    new Button()
                        .Text("Another Button to Click")
                        .CenterHorizontal(),

                    new HorizontalStackLayout
                    {
                        Spacing = 15,
                        HorizontalOptions = LayoutOptions.Center,
                        Children =
                        {
                            new Button()
                                .Text("Button 1"),

                            new Button()
                                .Text("Button 2"),
```

```
                        new Button()
                            .Text("Button 3")
                    }
                }
            }
        };
    }
}
}
```

Next, edit the *AppShell.xaml* file to add the new shell content element for the second page:

```
<?xml version="1.0" encoding="UTF-8" ?>
<Shell
    x:Class="StyleDemo.AppShell"

.

.

    <ShellContent
        Title="Home"
        ContentTemplate="{DataTemplate local:MainPage}"
        Route="MainPage" />

    <ShellContent
        Title="Implicit Styles"
        ContentTemplate="{DataTemplate local:SecondPage}"
        Route="SecondPage" />
</Shell>
```

Run the app, use the navigation menu to switch to the Implicit Styles page, and verify that the layout matches that shown in Figure 15-3:

Figure 15-3

Now that the layout of the second page is complete, we are ready to add some implicit styles. This involves creating a ResourceDictionary instance containing the style declarations and assigning it to the page's Resources property. Continue modifying the *SecondPage.cs* file so that it reads as follows:

```
public SecondPage()
{
    Resources = new ResourceDictionary
    {
        new Style<Button>()
            .Add(Button.FontSizeProperty, 32)
            .Add(Button.BorderColorProperty, Colors.Black)
            .Add(Button.BorderWidthProperty, 3)
            .Add(Button.CornerRadiusProperty, 20),

        new Style<Label>()
            .Add(Label.FontSizeProperty, 24)
            .Add(Label.FontAttributesProperty, FontAttributes.Italic |
                    FontAttributes.Bold)
    };

    Content = new VerticalStackLayout
    .
    .
```

The new resource dictionary contains styles that will apply to Button and Label controls at runtime. Affected Buttons will be rendered with a black border with rounded corners using a 32pt text size. Label text, on the other hand, will be displayed using a 24pt font with bold and italic attributes. Running the app should result in the layout shown below:

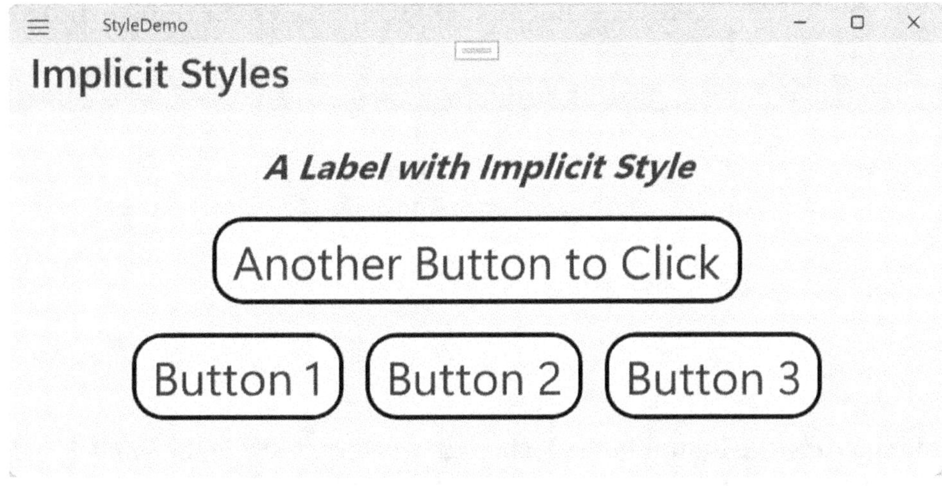


Figure 15-4

Working with Styling and Fonts

With this single declaration, all buttons in the current context adopt the same look and feel unless explicitly overridden. With the app still running, switch to the Main page and verify that the implicit styles were applied only to the controls on the second page.

To apply the implicit styles to the entire app, we must declare them at the Application level. To do so, copy and remove the resource dictionary declaration from *SecondPage.cs* and move it to the *App.xaml.cs* file as outlined below:

```
using CommunityToolkit.Maui.Markup;

namespace StyleDemo
{
    public partial class App : Application
    {
        public App()
        {
            InitializeComponent();

            Resources = new ResourceDictionary
            {
                new Style<Button>()
                    .Add(Button.FontSizeProperty, 32)
                    .Add(Button.BorderColorProperty, Colors.Black)
                    .Add(Button.BorderWidthProperty, 3)
                    .Add(Button.CornerRadiusProperty, 20),

                new Style<Label>()
                    .Add(Label.FontSizeProperty, 24)
                    .Add(Label.FontAttributesProperty,
                        FontAttributes.Italic | FontAttributes.Bold)
            };
        }

        protected override Window CreateWindow(
                        IActivationState? activationState)
        {
            return new Window(new AppShell());
        }
    }
}
```

Next time the app runs, the Button in the Main page will appear using the implicit style. You will also notice that while the options in the navigation menu have also adopted the implicit Label style, the Main page Label does not. This is because we are overriding the implicit style with the explicit headerStyle:

```
new Label()
    .Text("A Label with Style")
    .CenterHorizontal()
    .Style(headerStyle)
```

Remove the Style() extension method call, and this Label too will adopt the application-wide implicit style:

Figure 15-5

In addition to using resource dictionaries to add groups of global styles, it is also possible to apply individual styles to the current resource dictionary:

```
Resources.Add(
    new Style<Label>(l => l
        .FontFamily("OpenSansRegular")
        .TextColor(Colors.Black)
        .FontSize(16))
);
```

Before continuing, reapply the Style() extension method call to the Label:

```
new Label()
    .Text("A Label with Style")
    .CenterHorizontal()
    .Style(headerStyle)
```

## 15.5 Style Inheritance

Large applications often require groups of related styles. Style inheritance allows one style to be based on another, inheriting shared values while modifying or extending them. For example:

```
var baseLabel = new Style<Label>(l => l
    .FontSize(14)
    .TextColor(Colors.Gray));
```

```
var titleLabel = new Style<Label>(baseLabel, l => l
    .FontAttributes(FontAttributes.Bold)
    .FontSize(20)
    .TextColor(Colors.DarkSlateBlue));
```

Here, titleLabel builds upon baseLabel, inheriting its font and color but overriding certain properties. This approach mirrors the cascading principles familiar from web CSS but remains strongly typed and checked at compile time.

## 15.6 Using Resources and Dynamic Styling

Beyond styles, .NET MAUI provides a resource system for defining reusable constants such as colors, font sizes, dimensions, and image paths. Resources encourage centralization so that when your brand color or font family changes, you can update one location, and the entire app adapts.

In C# Markup, resources can be created directly in code without XAML:

```
Application.Current.Resources = new ResourceDictionary
{
    ["PrimaryColor"] = Colors.SteelBlue,
    ["AccentColor"]  = Colors.Coral,
    ["HeaderFontSize"] = 22,
    ["CornerRadiusSmall"] = 6
};
```

Each entry acts like a named constant accessible anywhere in the visual tree. These resources can be static (fixed at load time) or dynamic (updateable at runtime).

| Resource Type | Updates at Runtime | Typical Use Case |
| --- | --- | --- |
| StaticResource | No | Fixed sizes, spacing, fonts |
| DynamicResource | Yes | Theme colors, user settings, live preferences |

Table 15-1

Static resources are resolved once when the control is created and are applied using the Resource() extension method:

```
new Label()
    .Text("Accent Text")
    .Resource(Label.TextColorProperty, "AccentColor")
```

Dynamic resources, by contrast, remain connected to the dictionary so that when their values change, every bound control updates immediately:

```
new Label()
    .Text("Accent Text")
    .DynamicResource(Label.TextColorProperty, "AccentColor");
```

If AccentColor is changed (for example, by switching from light to dark mode), all labels using that dynamic resource are automatically redrawn with the new color.

## 15.7 Merged Resource Dictionaries

As your application grows, resource organization becomes crucial. Instead of maintaining one enormous dictionary, you can divide resources by theme or component:

```
public class ColorsResourceDictionary : ResourceDictionary
{
    public ColorsResourceDictionary()
    {
        Add("PrimaryColor", Colors.Blue);
        Add("SecondaryColor", Colors.LightGray);
    }
}


public class FontsResourceDictionary : ResourceDictionary
{
    public FontsResourceDictionary()
    {
        Add("TitleFontSize", 24);
        Add("BodyFontSize", 14);
    }
}


Resources = new ResourceDictionary();

Resources.MergedDictionaries.Add(new ColorsResourceDictionary());
Resources.MergedDictionaries.Add(new FontsResourceDictionary());
```

## 15.8 Resource Resolution Order

When working with styles, it helps to understand how .NET MAUI resolves resource lookups. When a control requests a resource, the framework searches upward through the visual hierarchy:

1. The control's own Resources

2. The containing Page or Layout Resources

3. The Application-level Resources

4. Merged dictionaries

This cascading lookup enables easy local overrides of global resources, providing fine-grained control while maintaining global consistency.

## 15.9 Working with Fonts

So far, we have focused primarily on color and font attribute style settings. An equally important area when implementing a consistent UI experience involves more than just font size and whether text is bold or italicized. Font styles also need to specify the font families that will be used to render the user interface text. Before we can reference specific fonts in our styles, we must first register them when the app is initialized. Registration of fonts is usually performed in the *MauiProgram.cs* file by calling the ConfigureFonts() instance of the MauiApp builder instance. In fact, the *MauiProgram.cs* file generated for us by Visual Studio when we created the project already contains the following code to register two fonts:

```
.
.
public static MauiApp CreateMauiApp()
{
    var builder = MauiApp.CreateBuilder();
    builder
        .UseMauiApp<App>()
        .UseMauiCommunityToolkitMarkup()
        .ConfigureFonts(fonts =>
        {
            fonts.AddFont("OpenSans-Regular.ttf", "OpenSansRegular");
            fonts.AddFont("OpenSans-Semibold.ttf", "OpenSansSemibold");
        });
.
.
}
```

The ConfigureFonts() lambda is passed a FontCollection object containing the list of registered fonts, on which we can call the AddFont() method to register additional fonts. The first argument to AddFont() is the name of the file containing the font, and the second is the alias by which we will reference the font in our UI code and style declarations.

## 15.10 Adding a New Font

Before we can register a new font and use it in our project, we must first download the font file, add it to our project resources, and reference it in the project configuration (.csproj) file. To demonstrate this in our project, we will download Google's Lato font. Begin by opening a browser window and navigating to the following web page:

*https://fonts.google.com/specimen/Lato*

Click the "Get Font" button to download the zipped font package, then use Windows File Explorer to extract all the files. Locate the Lato-Light.tff file, select it, and copy it by pressing Ctrl-C. Return to the Solution Explorer panel in Visual Studio and unfold the *Resources -> Fonts* tree node as shown in Figure 15-6 below:

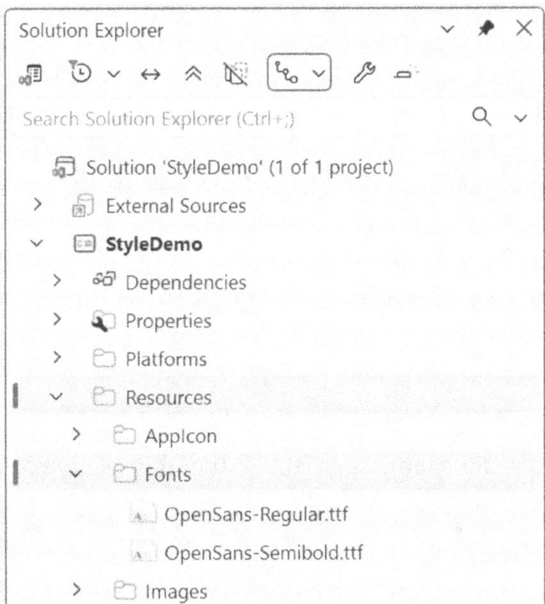

Figure 15-6

With the Fonts folder selected, press Ctrl-V to paste the Lato-Light.tff file into the folder:

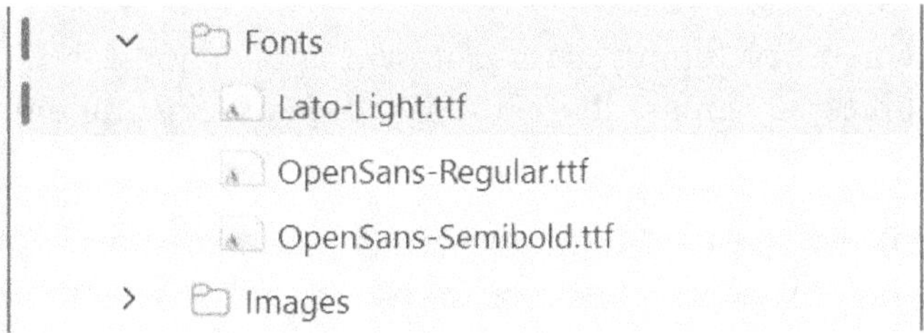

Figure 15-7

Next, right-click on the StyleDemo project at the top of the Solution Explorer tree and select the "Edit Project File" menu option. When the *StyleDemo.csproj* file loads into the editor, locate the Custom Fonts section and confirm that all of the font files in the Resources\Fonts folder are included in the project:

```
<!-- Custom Fonts -->
<MauiFont Include="Resources\Fonts\*" />
```

## 15.11 Registering and Using the New Font

To register the font, edit the *MauiProgram.cs* file and add it to the font collection as shown below:

```
var builder = MauiApp.CreateBuilder();
builder
    .UseMauiApp<App>()
    .UseMauiCommunityToolkitMarkup()
    .ConfigureFonts(fonts =>
    {
```

```
        fonts.AddFont("OpenSans-Regular.ttf", "OpenSansRegular");
        fonts.AddFont("OpenSans-Semibold.ttf", "OpenSansSemibold");
        fonts.AddFont("Lato-Light.ttf", "LatoLight");
    });
```

The final step before testing the app is to add the new font to the headerStyle declaration in the *MainPage.cs* file:

```
var headerStyle = new Style<Label>()
    .Add(Label.FontFamilyProperty, "LatoLight")
    .Add(Label.FontSizeProperty, 32)
    .
    .
    .
```

Rerun the app and check that the MainPage Label control appears using the Lato-Light font:

Figure 15-8

## 15.12 Platform-Specific Styling

For fine-tuning styles when developing cross-platform applications, .NET MAUI also supports platform-specific resources so apps adhere to native platform guidelines on iOS, Android, Windows, and macOS.

You can use conditional logic in C# Markup to apply platform-specific styles by accessing the Platform property of the DeviceInfo instance and comparing it to the values defined in the DevicePlatform structure. For example:

```
var button = new Label()
    .Text("My Button");



if (DeviceInfo.Platform == DevicePlatform.iOS)
    button.Font(size: 18, bold: true);
else if (DeviceInfo.Platform == DevicePlatform.Android)
    button.Font(size: 55, italic: true);
else if (DeviceInfo.Platform == DevicePlatform.WinUI)
    button.Font(size: 90, italic: true);
else if (DeviceInfo.Platform == DevicePlatform.macOS)
    button.Font(size: 55, italic: true);
```

## 15.13 Summary

This chapter introduced styling within .NET MAUI using C# Markup. It began by examining how to construct styles with fluent extensions and the distinction between explicit and implicit styles, including inheritance for creating families of related appearances. Next, it explored the use of resource dictionaries to store style properties centrally, contrasted static and dynamic resources, and introduced merged dictionaries for scalability. We also learned how to add fonts to a project and use them in style declarations.

# 16. Building Reusable Composite Components

Reusable UI components are essential to creating scalable, maintainable applications in .NET MAUI. As an application grows beyond its initial screens, repeated interface patterns inevitably occur. Without planning, these patterns must be re-created across multiple pages, increasing the maintenance burden and fragmenting the app's visual consistency. Composition allows developers to build small, focused UI building blocks that can be assembled throughout the application while retaining consistent layout, appearance, and behavior.

In C# Markup, reusable UI components are expressed entirely in code, providing a clear separation between the internal component structure and external configuration. This chapter examines how to create layout-based reusable UI components using composition, how to expose configurable behavior, and how to determine the appropriate level of abstraction for long-term maintainability.

## 16.1 Understanding UI Composition

Composition refers to the concept of assembling multiple controls into a single reusable container. Rather than deriving from a built-in control, you define a new class, typically inheriting from ContentView, combined with a layout such as VerticalStackLayout or Grid, populated with child elements. The resulting component becomes a standalone unit that encapsulates both presentation and optional behavior.

This approach is particularly well-suited to UI patterns that combine several controls. For example, a "profile card" typically includes an image, text labels, and a button. By composing these elements inside a custom class, you ensure that every profile card in the app maintains a uniform layout and behavior.

Figure 16-1 below is a simple conceptual diagram of how a composite component encapsulates multiple child elements:



Figure 16-1

Building Reusable Composite Components

The composite class becomes a semantic UI unit. Instead of scattering layout code across multiple pages, developers can instantiate ProfileCardView as a single control and configure its public properties.

## 16.2 Creating the CompositeDemo Project

Start Visual Studio and create a new project named CompositeDemo using the MauiMarkup project template.

## 16.3 Creating a Composite UI Component

The most common base class for composite components is ContentView. It provides a simple container for any layout structure and cleanly encapsulates internal composition. The reusable component we will create is a composite class similar to the ProfileCardView component outlined in Figure 16-1 above. The finished component will consist of two Labels, an Image, and a Button arranged within a Grid layout. Use the Solution Explorer to add a new class file named *ProfileCardView.cs* and implement the component as follows:

```
using CommunityToolkit.Maui.Markup;


namespace CompositeDemo
{
    public partial class ProfileCardView : ContentView
    {
        readonly Image _photo;
        readonly Label _nameLabel;
        readonly Label _titleLabel;
        readonly Button _contactButton;

        public ProfileCardView()
        {
            _photo = new Image
            {
                HeightRequest = 120,
                WidthRequest = 120

            }
            .Aspect(Aspect.AspectFit)
            .CenterHorizontal();

            _nameLabel = new Label()
                .Font(size: 20, bold: true)
                .TextColor(Colors.Black);

            _titleLabel = new Label()
```

```csharp
            .Font(size: 14)
            .TextColor(Colors.Gray);

        _contactButton = new Button()
            .Text("Contact")
            .Font(size: 14)
            .BackgroundColor(Colors.SteelBlue)
            .TextColor(Colors.White);

        Content = new Grid
        {
            Padding = 20,
            RowSpacing = 10,
            ColumnSpacing = 10,
            RowDefinitions =
            {
                new RowDefinition(GridLength.Auto),
                new RowDefinition(GridLength.Auto),
                new RowDefinition(GridLength.Auto)
            },
            ColumnDefinitions =
            {
                new ColumnDefinition(GridLength.Auto),
                new ColumnDefinition(GridLength.Auto)
            },
            Children =
            {
                _photo.Row(0).Column(0).RowSpan(3),
                _nameLabel.Row(0).Column(1),
                _titleLabel.Row(1).Column(1),
                _contactButton.Row(3).Column(1)
            }
        };
    }
}
```

Now that we have declared a composite component, we can use it in the *MainPage.cs* file as follows:

```csharp
using CommunityToolkit.Maui.Markup;

namespace CompositeDemo
{
```

```
public partial class MainPage : ContentPage
{
    public MainPage()
    {
        Content = new VerticalStackLayout
        {
            Children =
            {
                new ProfileCardView()
            }
        };
    }
}
```

Although the component contains all of visual elements required for our profile card, when we run the app, only the Button is visible:

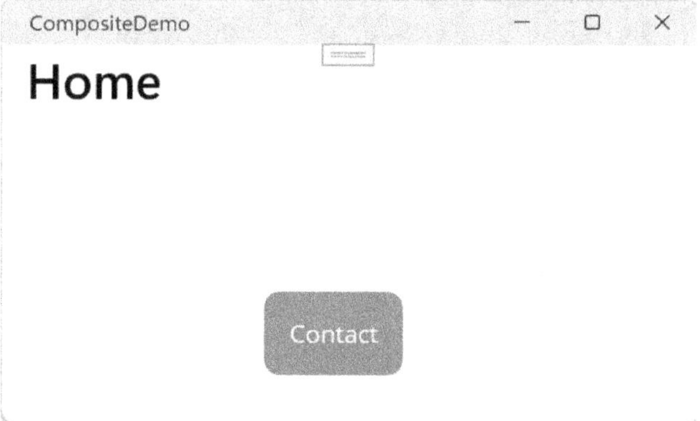


Figure 16-2

The other controls are present in the layout, but we have yet to apply any properties that would make them visible. These properties were undefined in the composite component declaration because we won't know which contact details to display until we create the ProfileCardView instances in the app. For the component to be useful, therefore, we need a way to make it configurable.

## 16.4 Adding Configurable Properties

While composite components should not expose their internal UI elements, they become far more powerful when they expose public properties that modify their internal state. .NET MAUI encourages this through dependency properties or regular .NET properties. Return to the *ProfileCardView.cs* file and add public properties for the Label text and Image source values:

```
using CommunityToolkit.Maui.Markup;

namespace CompositeDemo
{
```

```csharp
public partial class ProfileCardView : ContentView
{
    readonly Image _photo;
    readonly Label _nameLabel;
    readonly Label _titleLabel;
    readonly Button _contactButton;

    public string Name
    {
        get => _nameLabel.Text;
        set => _nameLabel.Text = value;
    }

    public string Title
    {
        get => _titleLabel.Text;
        set => _titleLabel.Text = value;
    }

    public ImageSource Photo
    {
        get => _photo.Source;
        set => _photo.Source = value;
    }
    .
    .
    .
}
```

Next, add code to set the properties on the ProfileCardView instance in the *MainPage.cs* file:

```csharp
public MainPage()
{
    Content = new VerticalStackLayout
    {
        Children =
        {
            new ProfileCardView
            {
                Name = "Jason Wilson",
                Title = "President & Chief Executive Officer",
                Photo = "dotnet_bot.png"
            }
        }
```

```
    };
}
```

This time when the app runs it will be populated with the contact information we provided:

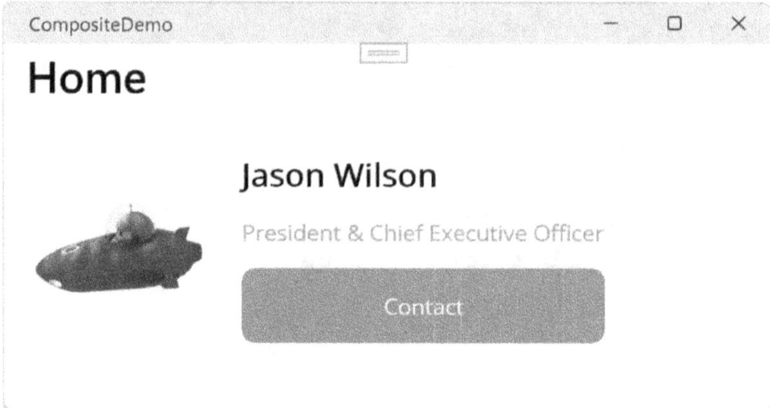


Figure 16-3

## 16.5 Encapsulating Interactive Behavior

Composite components often include interactions. Interactive behavior is added to components by declaring event properties for specific types of action, such as a button tap or the motion of a slider. These properties are then used to add and remove the external code to be executed when the event is triggered. As an example, modify the ProfileCardView declaration to add an event handler to handle Contact button clicks:

```
using CommunityToolkit.Maui.Markup;

namespace CompositeDemo
{
    public partial class ProfileCardView : ContentView
    {
        readonly Image _photo;
        readonly Label _nameLabel;
        readonly Label _titleLabel;
        readonly Button _contactButton;

        public event EventHandler ContactTapped
        {
            add => _contactButton.Clicked += value;
            remove => _contactButton.Clicked -= value;
        }
.

.
```

After adding the event to the component, we can add an event handler to the Contact button in the MainPage() method. This is achieved using the Invoke() method as outlined in the *"Views, Controls, and Event Handling"* chapter:

```csharp
public MainPage()
{
    Content = new VerticalStackLayout
    {
        Children =
        {
            new ProfileCardView
            {
                Name = "Jason Wilson",
                Title = "President & Chief Executive Officer",
                Photo = "dotnet_bot.png"
            }
            .Invoke(p =>
            {
                p.ContactTapped += OnButtonClicked;
            })
        }
    };

    static void OnButtonClicked(object? sender, EventArgs e)
    {
        if (sender is Button button)
        {
            button.Text("Connecting to Contact");
        }
    }
}
```

Next time the app runs, clicking the Contact button will trigger the event handler and change its text to "Connecting to Contact".

## 16.6 Summary

Composition provides a mechanism for building reusable UI components in .NET MAUI. These self-contained classes eliminate duplication, reinforce consistent design patterns, and maintain clean separation between layout, behavior, and application logic. Composite components serve as an essential bridge between low-level controls and higher-level pages, providing a flexible, maintainable way to build complex interfaces entirely in C# Markup.

In the next chapter, we will examine a different kind of reuse: extending and customizing .NET MAUI's built-in controls through inheritance to build flexible, data-aware custom UI elements.

# 17. Creating Custom Controls

While composing UI elements into reusable composite layout components is effective for many scenarios, there are cases where reusing or extending behavior at the control level is more appropriate. In these cases, creating custom controls, which are classes derived from a built-in control such as Button, Entry, or Label, provides an efficient way to encapsulate new capabilities or refine existing ones.

Custom controls allow developers to establish consistent visual patterns across the application, introduce new bindable properties, and implement custom interaction logic. This chapter explores how to create custom controls in .NET MAUI using C# Markup, how to introduce new bindable properties, and design controls that integrate cleanly into MVVM-based applications.

## 17.1 Understanding Custom Controls

Unlike composite components, which combine existing controls into new components, custom controls extend or enhance a single existing control to change its behavior or appearance. Custom controls are more advanced and are typically used when the functionality of a built-in control needs refinement beyond what can be achieved through composition or styles alone. Custom controls can add new commands or events, introduce new properties, and apply styling to existing controls.

## 17.2 Creating the CustomControlDemo Project

Start Visual Studio and create a new project named CustomControlDemo using the MauiMarkup project template.

## 17.3 Extending a Built-In Control

The simplest custom control derives from a single .NET MAUI control and adjusts its default appearance or behavior. Consider, for example, the requirement for a BoxView with a specific background color, size, and corner radius displayed in multiple locations throughout an app's user interface. One option would be to fully declare and customize a standard BoxView each time we need it:

```
new BoxView
{
    HeightRequest = 200,
    WidthRequest = 200,
    Color = Colors.DarkViolet,
    CornerRadius = 30
}
```

Alternatively we can create a custom control derived from the BoxView class and pre-configured

Creating Custom Controls

with the required properties. With the CustomControlDemo project loaded into Visual Studio, use the Solution Explorer to add a new class file named *RgbBoxView.cs*. Load the file into the code editor and modify it as follows:

```
namespace CustomControlDemo;

public partial class RgbBoxView : BoxView
{
    public RgbBoxView()
    {
        WidthRequest = 200;
        HeightRequest = 200;
        CornerRadius = 30;
        BackgroundColor = Colors.DarkViolet;
    }
}
```

Try out the custom BoxView by adding it to the MainPage layout in the *MainPage.cs* file:

```
public MainPage()
{
    Content = new VerticalStackLayout
    {
        Padding = 20,
        Spacing = 15,

        Children =
        {
            new RgbBoxView()
                .CenterHorizontal()
        }
    };
}
```

When rendered, the custom button will appear as shown in Figure 17-1 below:

Figure 17-1

# 17.4 Adding Bindable Properties

Many custom controls require new properties that integrate with .NET MAUI's binding system. Bindable properties allow external code to bind view-model values to your control while enabling the control to react automatically when those values change, a topic we covered in detail in *"MVVM and Data Binding in C# Markup"*.

To add bindable properties to a custom control, we declare them as BindableProperty instances, which we create by calling the BindableProperty.Create() method as follows:

```
BindableProperty.Create(
    propertyName,
    returnType,
    declaringType,
    defaultValue = null,
    defaultBindingMode,
    validateValue,
    propertyChanged,
    propertyChanging,
    coerceValue,
    defaultValueCreator
);
```

The purpose of each parameter is as follows:

- **propertyName** - The name of the property as a string (usually nameof(MyProperty)).

- **returnType** - Defines what kind of value this property can store and bind.

- **declaringType** - The class that owns the property (e.g., typeof(MyControl)).

- **defaultValue** - Initial value assigned before the user sets a value.

- **defaultBindingMode**- How bindings behave if the binding mode isn't specified (OneWay, TwoWay, etc.).

- **validateValue** - Code to be executed before the property accepts a new value. Useful for validation.

- **propertyChanged** - Code to be executed after the property value has changed. Used to update the UI, trigger events etc.

- **propertyChanging**- Code to be executed before the value changes.

- **coerceValue** - Changes the incoming value before it is stored.

- **defaultValueCreator** - Generates a dynamic default value at runtime.

Many of the options outlined above are optional when declaring a bindable property. The following, for example, is a BindableProperty that stores a Double numeric value belonging to our RgbBoxView control. It has a default value of 0.0 and calls a method named OnColorComponentChanged() when the underlying value changes:

```
public static readonly BindableProperty BlueProperty =
    BindableProperty.Create(
        nameof(Blue),
        typeof(double),
        typeof(RgbBoxView),
        0.0,
        propertyChanged: OnColorComponentChanged);
```

Once the bindable properties have been declared, we must also provide a matching Common Language Runtime (CLR) wrapper for each property.

## 17.5 Declaring CLR Property Wrappers

In .NET MAUI, a CLR property wrapper is the normal-looking C# property that you expose to developers so they can get and set the bindable properties in your custom controls using simple property syntax. Although the wrapper appears to be an ordinary C# property, it does not actually store its own value. Instead, it delegates all value storage and retrieval to the .NET MAUI framework using the methods GetValue() and SetValue(). The CLR wrapper for the example BlueProperty above would read as follows:

```
public double Blue
{
    get => (double)GetValue(BlueProperty);
    set => SetValue(BlueProperty, value);
}
```

Without the CLR wrapper, we would need to call SetValue on our custom control instance to reference the bindable property as follows:

```
myBox.SetValue(BlueProperty, 0.5);
```

Instead, the CLR wrapper allows us to access the property using normal C# property syntax:

```
myBox.Blue = 0.5;
```

## 17.6 A Bindable Properties Example

To demonstrate the bindable properties, we will add three properties to our RgbBoxView control representing red, green, and blue (RGB) color values, which will, in turn, control the background color of the box.

Make the following changes to the *RgbBoxView.cs* file to add the bindable properties and to remove the original color property:

```
namespace CustomControlDemo;

public partial class RgbBoxView : BoxView
{
```

```csharp
public RgbBoxView()
{
    WidthRequest = 200;
    HeightRequest = 200;
    CornerRadius = 30;
    BackgroundColor = Colors.DarkViolet;
}


public static readonly BindableProperty RedProperty =
    BindableProperty.Create(
        nameof(Red),
        typeof(double),
        typeof(RgbBoxView),
        0.0,
        propertyChanged: OnColorComponentChanged);

public static readonly BindableProperty GreenProperty =
    BindableProperty.Create(
        nameof(Green),
        typeof(double),
        typeof(RgbBoxView),
        0.0,
        propertyChanged: OnColorComponentChanged);

public static readonly BindableProperty BlueProperty =
    BindableProperty.Create(
        nameof(Blue),
        typeof(double),
        typeof(RgbBoxView),
        0.0,
        propertyChanged: OnColorComponentChanged);
}
```

Next, add the corresponding CLR property wrappers to the class:

```csharp
public partial class RgbBoxView : BoxView
{
    .

    .

    public double Red
    {
        get => (double)GetValue(RedProperty);
        set => SetValue(RedProperty, value);
```

```
    }

    public double Green
    {
        get => (double)GetValue(GreenProperty);
        set => SetValue(GreenProperty, value);
    }

    public double Blue
    {
        get => (double)GetValue(BlueProperty);
        set => SetValue(BlueProperty, value);
    }

    .
    .
    .
```

The propertyChanged parameter of each bindable property is configured to call a method named OnColorComponentChanged() when the underlying property value changes. Within this method, we will update the color of the box with the current RGB values as follows:

```
public partial class RgbBoxView : BoxView
{

    .

    .

    private static void OnColorComponentChanged(BindableObject bindable,
                                        object oldValue, object newValue)
    {
        if (bindable is RgbBoxView box)
        {
            box.UpdateColor();
        }
    }

    private void UpdateColor()
    {
        Color = new Color((float)Red, (float)Green, (float)Blue);
    }
}
```

Add another class file, this time named *MainViewModel.cs*, declare it as an observable object and add observable properties for the RGB colors:

```
using CommunityToolkit.Mvvm.ComponentModel;

namespace CustomControlDemo
```

```
{
    public partial class MainViewModel : ObservableObject
    {
        [ObservableProperty]
        public partial double Red { get; set; }

        [ObservableProperty]
        public partial double Green { get; set; }

        [ObservableProperty]
        public partial double Blue { get; set; }
    }
}
```

Return to the *MainPage.cs* file and add three Slider controls to the existing layout, binding the slider values to the corresponding view model color properties, remembering also to initialize the view model and binding context:

```
public MainPage()
{
    var viewModel = new MainViewModel();
    BindingContext = viewModel;

    Content = new VerticalStackLayout
    {
        Padding = 20,
        Spacing = 15,

        Children =
        {
            new RgbBoxView()
                .CenterHorizontal(),

            new Slider
            {
                WidthRequest = 250,
                Minimum = 0,
                Maximum = 1,
                Value = 0.0
            }
            .BackgroundColor(Colors.Red)
            .Bind(Slider.ValueProperty, nameof(MainViewModel.Red)),
```

```
            new Slider
            {
                WidthRequest = 250,
                Minimum = 0,
                Maximum = 1,
                Value = 0.0
            }
            .BackgroundColor(Colors.Green)
            .Bind(Slider.ValueProperty, nameof(MainViewModel.Green)),

            new Slider
            {
                WidthRequest = 250,
                Minimum = 0,
                Maximum = 1,
                Value = 0.0
            }
            .BackgroundColor(Colors.Blue)
            .Bind(Slider.ValueProperty, nameof(MainViewModel.Blue))
        }
    };
}
```

As the final step, bind our RgbBoxView color values to the view model color properties:

```
public MainPage()
{
    var viewModel = new MainViewModel();
    BindingContext = viewModel;

    Content = new VerticalStackLayout
    {
        Children =
        {
            new RgbBoxView()
                .Bind(RgbBoxView.RedProperty, nameof(MainViewModel.Red))
                .Bind(RgbBoxView.GreenProperty,
                          nameof(MainViewModel.Green))
                .Bind(RgbBoxView.BlueProperty,
                          nameof(MainViewModel.Blue))
                .CenterHorizontal(),
```

Run the app and verify that the box color changes in response to slider adjustments:

Figure 17-2

## 17.7 Summary

Custom controls are an important complement to layout-based reusable components. By deriving from built-in .NET MAUI controls, you can introduce consistent styling, encapsulate behavior, and create new bindable properties that integrate seamlessly with the application's data and command structure. These controls are especially valuable when behavior or styling is conceptually tied to a single control rather than a collection of elements.

Throughout this chapter, we explored how to refine built-in controls through inheritance and how to create bindable properties for MVVM-based configurations. In the next chapter, we will further extend these ideas, exploring advanced component patterns using generics and fluent APIs.

# 18. Generic Components

In the chapter *"Building Reusable Composite Components"*, we created custom components by assembling multiple views and configuration settings into a single reusable container. Although these components provided some flexibility—such as changing a button's color or specifying a label's text—the structure of the encapsulated views remained fixed. Generic components extend this idea of reusability by allowing us to specify the views a component should contain when we create an instance of it, rather than when we define it. This chapter introduces generic components and demonstrates how they are created and used.

## 18.1 An Overview of UI Component Generics

When we build composite components, we decide in advance which views they will contain and how those views will be arranged. Generic components offer the same ability to bundle related views and behavior, but also allow us to define placeholders that can be populated with any view we choose when we use the component in our UI code. This approach allows us to design UI components that combine predefined structure with interchangeable view elements.

Consider a composite component composed of three Label views arranged vertically in a stack layout. By exposing configurable properties, we can adjust component aspects at runtime—for example, changing the label text or the font size. Despite these customizations, however, the component remains limited to displaying a vertical stack containing three Label controls. No matter how flexible the configuration becomes, the structure itself is fixed.

Suppose, however, that we need to display three vertically stacked views, but do not know which view will occupy the middle position until the component is instantiated. In the composite component's current form, the middle element must always be the Label declared at design time, leaving no opportunity to substitute a different view. The solution is to convert the middle element into a *placeholder* that can be filled with any view we choose when creating the component instance. This is precisely the flexibility that generic components provide.

## 18.2 Declaring Generic Components

Generic components are declared in much the same way as composite components, except that they are configured to accept one or more placeholder parameters. These placeholders represent views that will be supplied when the component is instantiated rather than when it is declared.

The following code illustrates the basic syntax of a generic component definition:

```
public partial class ExampleGeneric<T1, T2, T3, ...> : ContentView
    where T1 : Paramater-Type, new()
    where T2 : Parameter-Type, new()
    where T3 : ...
{
```

```
    readonly T1 _viewOne;
    readonly T2 _viewTwo;
    readonly T3 ...


    public ExampleGeneric()
    {
        _viewOne = new T1();
        _viewTwo = new T2();
  .

  .

        Content = new Layout-Component
        {
            Children =
            {
                _viewOne,
                _viewTwo,
  .

  .


            }
        };
    }
}
```

For type safety, a placeholder parameter can be declared with a specific view type, such as Label, Button, or Entry, ensuring that only views of that type can be passed to the component. Alternatively, declaring a parameter as View allows any view type to be used there. In the following example, the view supplied for the T1 placeholder must be a Label, while the T2 placeholder accepts any view derived from View:

```
public partial class ExampleGeneric<T1, T2> : ContentView
    where T1 : Label, new()
    where T2 : View, new()
{
  .

  .

```

Caution should be used when declaring View-type parameters. Declaring a placeholder parameter as a specific view type provides strong compile-time guarantees, ensuring that only appropriate views can be passed to the component. When a parameter is declared simply as View, however, that safety net disappears, although this offers greater flexibility, it also increases the risk of unintended types being supplied, potentially leading to runtime errors if the component logic assumes properties or behaviors that are not shared by all views.

Once a generic component has been declared, it can be instantiated like any other component. In the example below, we create an instance of our example generic component and supply a Label and a Picker to populate its placeholders:

```
public MainPage()
{
    Content = new ExampleGeneric<Label, Picker>
    {
        .

        .

    };
}
```

## 18.3 Preparing the GenericDemo Project

To demonstrate generic components in practice, we will extend the ProfileCardView composite component created in an earlier chapter by adding a placeholder. Begin by locating the CompositeDemo project in File Explorer, making a copy named GenericDemo, and opening the new project in Visual Studio.

In its current form, ProfileCardView is limited to displaying a contact's information. Suppose, however, that we need a version that allows the user to edit and save those details. One approach would be to create a second component that duplicates much of the original but replaces the Label views with editable controls. A more flexible solution is to transform ProfileCardView into a generic component, allowing us to substitute either Label controls or editable views for the contact name and job title as needed.

In the remainder of this chapter, we will adapt ProfileCardView by converting the name and title labels into placeholders. Before we do that, we must first make the button text configurable so that its purpose can change depending on how the card is used. Open the *ProfileCardView.cs* file and add a new configuration property for the button text:

```
public partial class ProfileCardView<TContactName, TContactTitle> :
ContentView
    where TContactName : Entry, new()
    where TContactTitle : View, new()
{
    .


    .

    public event EventHandler ContactTapped
    {
        add => _contactButton.Clicked += value;
        remove => _contactButton.Clicked -= value;
    }


    public string ButtonText
    {
        get => _contactButton.Text;
```

```
        set => _contactButton.Text = value;

    }
.
.
```

Next, locate the _contactButton initialization code, and remove the call to the Text() extension method:

```
_contactButton = new Button()
    .Text("Contact")
    .Font(size: 14)
    .BackgroundColor(Colors.SteelBlue)
    .TextColor(Colors.White);
```

## 18.4 Declaring the Placeholders

Remaining in the *ProfileCardView.cs* file, modify the class declaration to add two placeholder parameters and remove the two Label views as follows:

```
using CommunityToolkit.Maui.Markup;


namespace CompositeDemo
{
    public partial class ProfileCardView<TContactName, TContactTitle> :
                                                    ContentView
        where TContactName : Entry, new()
        where TContactTitle : View, new()
    {
        readonly Image _photo;
        readonly Label _nameLabel;
        readonly Label _titleLabel;
        readonly Button _contactButton;
        readonly TContactName _contactNameView;
        readonly TContactTitle _contactTitleView;
.
.
```

Note that the contact name placeholder is restricted to Entry views, while the contact title can be populated with any view type.

After removing the original Label views, the corresponding configurable property for the contact name must be updated to reference the new placeholder view. Also, since we can no longer guarantee that the type of view provided for the contact title placeholder will have a Text property, the Title configuration property must be removed:

```
.
.
public string Name
```

```
{
    get => _contactNameView.Text;
    set => _contactNameView.Text = value;
}
```

~~public string Title~~
~~{~~
~~    get => _titleLabel.Text;~~
~~    set => _titleLabel.Text = value;~~
~~}~~

## 18.5 Initializing the Placeholder Views

When we create a ProfileCardView instance, we will provide it with two view types, which we need to create within the body of our component. Once again, the now redundant Label views will be deleted:

```
public ProfileCardView()
{
    _photo = new Image
    {
        HeightRequest = 120,
        WidthRequest = 120

    }
    .Aspect(Aspect.AspectFit)
    .CenterHorizontal();
```

~~_nameLabel = new Label()~~
~~        .Font(size: 20, bold: true)~~
~~        .TextColor(Colors.Black);~~

~~_titleLabel = new Label()~~
~~        .Font(size: 14)~~
~~        .TextColor(Colors.Gray);~~

```
    _contactNameView = new TContactName();
    _contactTitleView = new TContactTitle();
```

Finally, replace the Label views in the Grid layout with the placeholder views:

Generic Components

```
Children =
{
    _photo.Row(0).Column(0).RowSpan(3),
    ~~_nameLabel.Row(0).Column(1),~~
    ~~_titleLabel.Row(1).Column(1),~~
    _contactNameView.Row(0).Column(1),
    _contactTitleView.Row(1).Column(1),
    _contactButton.Row(2).Column(1)
}
```

## 18.6 Using the Generic Component

With most of the work on the ProfileCardView component complete, we are ready to test it. Open the *MainPage.cs* file and make the changes outlined below. To allow some flexibility in configuring the component instance later in the chapter, we will perform the initialization outside the page's Content block and reference it via a variable. Also, take this opportunity to modify the button click event handler:

```
public partial class MainPage : ContentPage
{
    public MainPage()
    {
        var profileCard = new ProfileCardView<Entry, Entry>
        {
            Name = "Sarah Johnson",
            Photo = "dotnet_bot.png",
            ButtonText = "Save Contact"
        };

        Content = new VerticalStackLayout
        {
            Children =
            {
                ~~new ProfileCardView~~
                ~~{~~
                ~~Name = "Jason Wilson",~~
                ~~Title = "President & Chief Executive Officer",~~
                ~~Photo = "dotnet_bot.png"~~
                ~~}~~
                profileCard
                    .Invoke(p =>
                    {
                        p.ContactTapped += OnButtonClicked;
                    })
```

```
        }
    };
.
.
static void OnButtonClicked(object? sender, EventArgs e)
{
    if (sender is Button button)
    {
        button.Text("Contact Saved");
    }
}
```

Run the app and verify that the Entry views appear in place of the name and title Labels as illustrated in Figure 18-1 below:

Figure 18-1

Unfortunately, because we had to remove the Title configuration property from the component declaration, we cannot directly set the contact's job title text within the profile card initialization. To resolve this, we need to make the contact title placeholder view accessible as a configuration property in the ProfileCardView class:

```
public partial class ProfileCardView<TContactName, TContactTitle> :
ContentView
    where TContactName : Entry, new()
    where TContactTitle : View, new()
{
    readonly Image _photo;
    readonly Button _contactButton;
    readonly TContactName _contactNameView;
    readonly TContactTitle _contactTitleView;

    public TContactTitle TitleView
```

```
    {
        get => _contactTitleView;
    }
```

.

.

Return to the *MainPage.cs* file and add code to access the view and set the title text:

.

.

```
var profileCard = new ProfileCardView<Entry, Entry>
{
    Name = "Sarah Johnson",
    Photo = "dotnet_bot.png",
    ButtonText = "Save Contact"
};


profileCard.TitleView.Text = "Senior Software Engineer";
```

.

.

After restarting the app, the contact title Entry view will contain the title text:

Figure 18-2

## 18.7 Changing the Title Placeholder View

With the generic component completed, our last task is to verify that we can assign a different view type to the title placeholder. In this case, we will use a Picker control pre-configured with a list of job titles from which to make a selection. Edit the *MainPage.cs* file and make the following changes:

```
public MainPage()
{
    var profileCard = new ProfileCardView<Entry, Picker>
    {
```

```
        Name = "Sarah Johnson",
        Photo = "dotnet_bot.png",
        ButtonText = "Save Contact"
    };


    profileCard.TitleElement.Text = "Senior Software Engineer";


    profileCard.TitleView.ItemsSource = new List<string>
    {
        "Chief Technology Officer",
        "Chief Executive Officer",
        "Chief Operating Officer"
    };
    .
    .
```

Restart the app and click on the Picker to make a selection from the list of job titles:

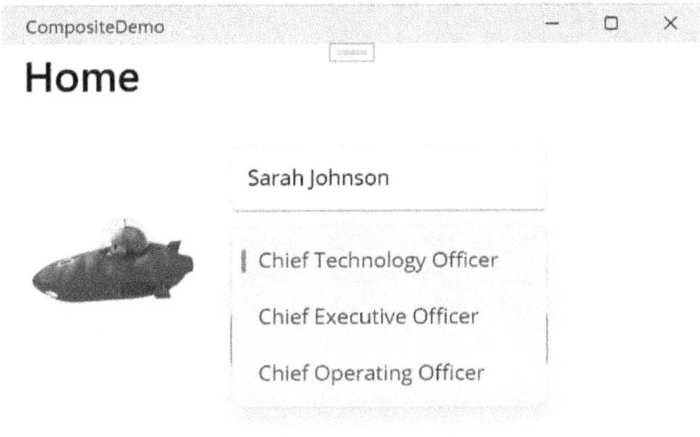

Figure 18-3

## 18.8 Summary

This chapter extended the concept of reusable composite components by introducing generic components. Unlike traditional composite components, which define their structure at design time, generic components allow specific views to be supplied when the component is instantiated. This was achieved by defining placeholder parameters constrained to particular view types, enabling both flexibility and type safety. By adapting the ProfileCardView component, we saw how placeholders can replace fixed elements, how these views are instantiated and integrated into the layout, and how they can be accessed and configured at runtime. By allowing interchangeable UI elements within a predefined structure, generic components provide a powerful way to build flexible, reusable user interface components.

# 19. Understanding Fluent APIs

"Fluent" is a word often associated with C# Markup, and it appears prominently in documentation and descriptions. Fluent APIs allow us to configure the appearance and behavior of views using a concise and declarative programming style. This chapter introduces fluent APIs in C# Markup and demonstrates how to add fluent support to your custom component properties.

## 19.1 Fluency and Extension Methods

Read just about any description of C# Markup, and you will find references to its *fluent* approach to app development. But what makes C# Markup "fluent"? A typical dictionary definition of "fluent" reads as follows:

*"Able to express oneself easily and articulately."*

In the context of C# Markup, this ease of expression is provided via its fluent API which consists of extension or helper methods that can be chained together and applied to UI views to define their appearance and behavior. These extension methods are essentially wrappers for the underlying view properties, making UI code more readable and concise.

We have been using the fluent API extensively in the preceding book chapters. A simple example that configures the text appearing on a Button view using the fluent programming style might read as follows:

```
new Button()
    .Text("Save Contact")
```

Moreover, we can chain extension method calls together, such as applying font, color, and corner radius properties to our Button view:

```
new Button()
    .Text("Save Contact")
    .BackgroundColor(Colors.SteelBlue)
    .TextColor(Colors.White)
    .CornerRadius(6)
```

The use of fluent API extension methods is usually optional, and the same results can often be achieved using view property setters, for example:

```
new Button
{
    Text = "Save Contact",
    BackgroundColor = Colors.SteelBlue,
    TextColor = Colors.White,
    CornerRadius = 6
```

```
}
```

In general, it is recommended to use an extension method when one is available instead of a property setter. That said, some core .NET MAUI properties do not have fluent extension methods, in which case, standard property setters or object initializers must be used. There are, for example, no extension method wrappers for the LineBreakMode and WidthRequest properties of the Label view, requiring the use of setters:

```
new Label
{
    LineBreakMode = LineBreakMode.WordWrap,
    WidthRequest = 1000
}
.Text("This is a long line of text that will wrap automatically.")
```

Extension methods and property setters are not mutually exclusive and, as in the case below, they are often combined when configuring a view:

```
new Label
{
    LineBreakMode = LineBreakMode.WordWrap,
    WidthRequest = 1000
}
.Text("This is a long line of text that will wrap automatically.")
```

## 19.2 Creating Custom Extension Methods

We know from experience that C# Markup provides fluent API wrappers for many of the core .NET MAUI components. In the rest of this chapter, we will explain how to add fluent API extension methods to custom components and generics properties. This is a relatively simple process consisting of making the properties publicly accessible, and writing the fluent extension methods to set the properties.

An extension method must be declared inside a static class and must itself be static. The first parameter, prefixed with the *this* keyword, specifies the type being extended. This parameter determines which type the method appears to belong to when used in client code, for example:

```
public static class ViewExtensions
{
    public static View SetSomething(this View view)
    {
        // configure view
        return view;
    }
}
```

Note that the extension method above is intended for use with custom component properties and returns the view instance to enable method chaining. The following variation of the example extension method has been modified to accept a string parameter:

```
public static class ViewExtensions
{
    public static View SetSomething(this View view, string text)
    {
        // use parameter
        return view;
    }
}
```

Custom extension methods may also be applied to generics. The following code, for example, declares an extension method for a generic property:

```
public static class CardExtensions
{
    public static Card<T1, T2> SetTitle<T1, T2>(
        this Card<T1, T2> card,
        string title)
        where T1 : View
        where T2 : View
    {

        return card;

    }

}
```

## 19.3 A Custom Fluent Extension Method Example

As a practical demonstration of custom extension methods, we will modify the GenericDemo project from the previous chapter. Begin by locating the GenericsDemo project in Windows File Explorer, making a copy named FluentAPIDemo, and opening the new project in Visual Studio.

We will begin by creating an extension method for the contact name property. To do so, the first task is to make the TContactName view component public so we can access it from within our extension method. We can also optionally delete the current setter property to enforce fluent configuration. Edit the *ProfileCardView.cs* file and make the following modifications:

```
namespace CompositeDemo
{
    public partial class ProfileCardView<TContactName, TContactTitle>
                                                : ContentView
        where TContactName : Entry, new()
        where TContactTitle : View, new()
    {

        readonly Image _photo;
        readonly Button _contactButton;
        readonly TContactName _contactNameView;
```

```
        readonly TContactTitle _contactTitleView;


    public TContactName NameView => _contactNameView;

.

.

        public string Name
        {
            get => _contactNameView.Text;
            set => _contactNameView.Text = value;
        }

.

.
```

Remaining within the *ProfileCardView.cs* file, add the extension class as follows:

```
using CommunityToolkit.Maui.Markup;

namespace CompositeDemo
{
    public partial class ProfileCardView<TContactName, TContactTitle> :
ContentView
        where TContactName : Entry, new()
        where TContactTitle : View, new()
    {
        readonly Image _photo;
        readonly Button _contactButton;
        readonly TContactName _contactNameView;
        readonly TContactTitle _contactTitleView;

.

.

    }


    public static class ProfileCardViewExtensions
    {
        public static ProfileCardView<TContactName, TContactTitle>
                ContactName<TContactName, TContactTitle>(
            this ProfileCardView<TContactName, TContactTitle> card,
            string name)
            where TContactName : Entry, new()
            where TContactTitle : View, new()
        {
            card.NameView.Text = name;
            return card;
```

```
        }
    }
}
```

The code above defines a generic extension method that provides fluent configuration support for setting the contact name on the ProfileCardView.

The ProfileCardViewExtensions class is declared static, as required for any class that contains extension methods. Inside it, the ContactName method is also static and generic, using the same type parameters (TContactName and TContactTitle) as the component it extends so that it works with any valid ProfileCardView instance.

The first parameter, *this ProfileCardView<TContactName, TContactTitle> card*, marks the method as an extension method, allowing it to be called using instance syntax such as ContactName("Jane Doe"):

```
public static ProfileCardView<TContactName, TContactTitle>
        ContactName<TContactName, TContactTitle>(
    this ProfileCardView<TContactName, TContactTitle> card,
    string name)
```

The generic constraints match those of the ProfileCardView component, ensuring the extension is compatible with all valid instantiations:

```
public static ProfileCardView<TContactName, TContactTitle>
ContactName<TContactName, TContactTitle>(
.

.

    where TContactName : Entry, new()
    where TContactTitle : View, new()
{
```

Inside the method, the provided name is assigned to the Text property of the exposed NameView, and the configured component is returned:

```
card.NameView.Text = name;
return card;.
```

Next, modify the ProfileCardView and extension class declarations to add an extension method for the photo property:

```
public partial class ProfileCardView<TContactName, TContactTitle> :
ContentView
    where TContactName : Entry, new()
    where TContactTitle : View, new()
{
    readonly Image _photo;
    readonly Button _contactButton;
    readonly TContactName _contactNameView;
```

```
    readonly TContactTitle _contactTitleView;

    public TContactName NameView => _contactNameView;
    public Image PhotoView => _photo;

    public TContactTitle TitleView
    {
        get => _contactTitleView;
    }

    .

    .

}


public static class ProfileCardViewExtensions
{
    public static ProfileCardView<TContactName, TContactTitle>
                        Photo<TContactName, TContactTitle>(
        this ProfileCardView<TContactName, TContactTitle> card,
        ImageSource source)
        where TContactName : Entry, new()
        where TContactTitle : View, new()
    {
        card.PhotoView.Source = source;
        return card;
    }

    public static ProfileCardView<TContactName, TContactTitle>
                        ContactName<TContactName, TContactTitle>(
        this ProfileCardView<TContactName, TContactTitle> card,

        .

        .

    }
}
```

With the fluent API changes complete, the code in *MainPage.cs* must be modified to replace the name and photo property setter code with calls to our new extension methods:

```
    .

    .

public MainPage()
{
    var profileCard = new ProfileCardView<Entry, Picker>
    {
```

```
    Name = "Sarah Johnson",
    Photo = "dotnet_bot.png",
    ButtonText = "Save Contact"
}
.ContactName("Jason Creighton")
.Photo("dotnet_bot.png");

.

.
```

Build and run the app to verify that the name and photo properties are set correctly, verifying that the extension methods are working.

## 19.4 Summary

Fluent APIs provide a way to express configuration and intent in code that reads naturally from left to right, closely resembling a sentence rather than a sequence of disconnected instructions. By returning the configured object and enabling method chaining, fluent APIs make code more concise and easier to understand. In UI frameworks such as .NET MAUI, fluent APIs are particularly valuable because they allow layout, styling, and behavior to be described declaratively in code without obscuring the underlying interface structure.

# 20. Navigation and Shell Integration

There are two goals for this chapter. The first is to fulfill our promise in the *"Building a C# Markup MAUI App"* chapter by migrating the AppShell from the *AppShell.xaml* file to C# code, and then explain how to implement navigation between an app's screens. Both these tasks, however, first require an understanding of the internal hierarchy of a .NET MAUI app.

## 20.1 The .NET MAUI Application Hierarchy

In the *"Building a C# Markup MAUI App"* chapter, we explored the *AppShell.xaml* file, which contains the Shell declaration for the project. Although we have transitioned away from XAML in other parts of our projects, we have yet to do so for the AppShell declaration. Before doing so, however, we need to take some time to outline the internal hierarchy of a typical .NET MAUI app. From a high-level perspective, the internal hierarchy is visualized in Figure 20-1:

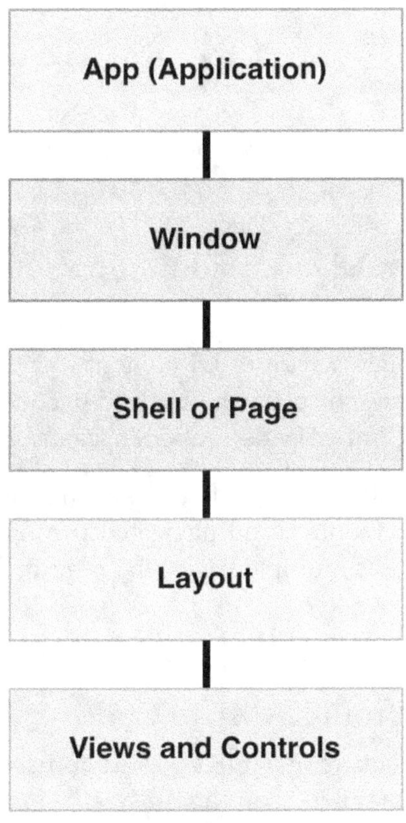


Figure 20-1

In the above hierarchy, the top-level App class (subclassed from the .NET MAUI core Application class) is responsible for the lifecycle of the running app, the resource dictionaries, and the creation and management of Window instances. A .NET MAUI app can only have one App instance. An app, however, can have multiple Window instances. Although mobile devices typically display a single window at a time, desktop and tablet platforms commonly allow multiple windows from the same application. A .NET MAUI app can therefore create multiple Window instances to display separate documents, support side-by-side workflows, or present utility interfaces such as settings or inspector panels. Each window maintains its own navigation stack and visual tree, allowing these interfaces to operate independently:

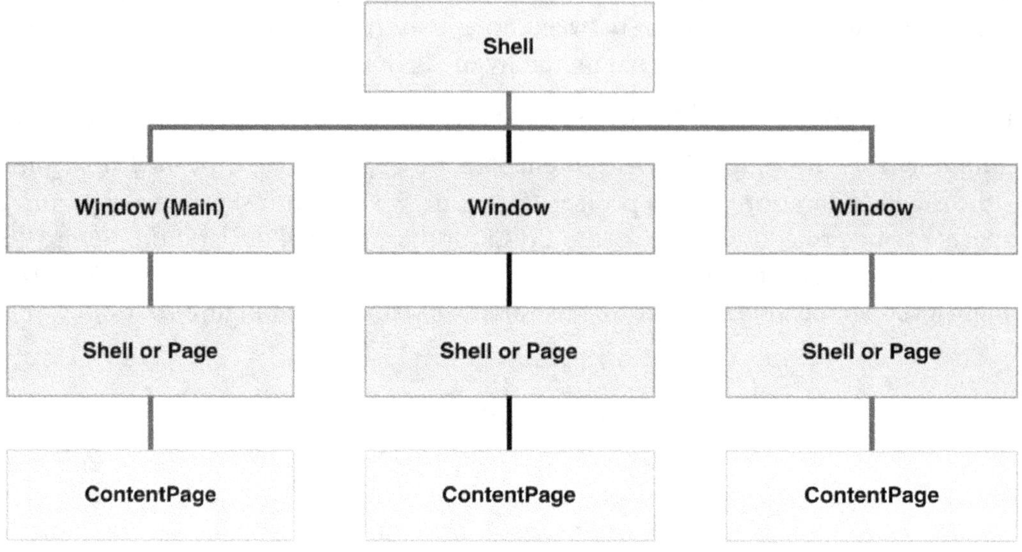


Figure 20-2

For the immediate child of the Window instance, we have a choice of declaring a Page or Shell instance:

- **Page** - A Page represents a single screen of UI content in a .NET MAUI application. It hosts the visual tree's layouts and views, displays the UI, and participates in navigation. Several Page types are available, including ContentPage, TabbedPage, and NavigationPage.

- **Shell** - A Shell instance is a specialized page that acts as the app's navigation container, defining how child Pages are organized, routed, and navigated throughout the app. Use a Shell as the Window child when your app has multiple Pages that require flexible navigation, including tab bar or flyout-based structures.

It is worth noting that AppShell is a subclass of Shell.

## 20.2 Moving the AppShell from XAML to Code

Now that we understand the structure of a .NET MAUI app and how the AppShell fits into this hierarchy, we can remove our dependency on the *AppShell.xaml* file.

In this chapter, we will work with a pre-created project named NavDemo, included with the project examples download via the link provided in the *"Introducing .NET MAUI and Declarative UI Design"* chapter.

NavDemo is a simple project created using our custom MAUIMarkup template and consists of three pages (MainPage, DetailPage and EditPage), to which we will add navigation support later in the chapter.

Open the NavDemo project and review the *App.xaml.cs* file which reads as follows:

```
namespace NavDemo
{
    public partial class App : Application
    {
        public App()
        {
            InitializeComponent();
        }

        protected override Window CreateWindow(
                    IActivationState? activationState)
        {
            return new Window(new AppShell());
        }
    }
}
```

The App class is a subclass of the .NET MAUI core Application class. It overrides the CreateWindow() method, which, in turn, returns a new Window initialized with an instance of the AppShell class declared in *AppShell.xaml*, the content of which reads as follows:

```
<?xml version="1.0" encoding="UTF-8" ?>
<Shell
    x:Class="NavDemo.AppShell"
    xmlns="http://schemas.microsoft.com/dotnet/2021/maui"
    xmlns:x="http://schemas.microsoft.com/winfx/2009/xaml"
    xmlns:local="clr-namespace:NavDemo"
    Title="NavDemo">

    <ShellContent
        Title="Home"
        ContentTemplate="{DataTemplate local:MainPage}"
        Route="MainPage" />
</Shell>
```

The code file associated with *AppShell.xaml* is named *AppShell.xaml.cs* and contains the following code:

```
namespace NavDemo
{
```

```
    public partial class AppShell : Shell
    {
        public AppShell()
        {
            InitializeComponent();
        }
    }
}
```

Right-click on *AppShell.xaml.cs* file in the Solution Explorer, select the "Open in File Explorer" menu option, and rename the file to *AppShell.cs*. Use the Solution Explorer to delete the *AppShell.xaml* file, then modify *AppShell.cs* to remove the XAML file initialization code:

```
namespace NavDemo
{
    public partial class AppShell : Shell
    {
        public AppShell()
        {
            InitializeComponent();
        }
    }
}
```

## 20.3 Navigation Models in .NET MAUI

Before looking at some examples, it helps to understand the navigation models available in .NET MAUI. At a high level, .NET MAUI supports two navigation approaches: stack-based and Shell-based.

Stack-based navigation is built around the concept of pushing and popping pages on a navigation stack. This approach is simple, predictable, and closely mirrors the mental model of moving forward and backward through screens. It is particularly well-suited to smaller applications or where navigation follows a linear path.

Shell-based navigation introduces a higher-level abstraction. It provides URI-based routing, visual containers such as flyout menus and tab bars, and built-in support for hierarchical navigation.

Both approaches are valid, and the choice between them depends on application complexity and architectural preferences.

## 20.4 A Stack-based Navigation Example

The simplest way to enable navigation in a .NET MAUI application is to wrap the main page in a NavigationPage. This establishes a navigation stack and enables calls to the PushAsync() and PopAsync() methods of the Navigation property. For example, to navigate to a new page, a call is made to PushAsync() passing through as an argument an instance of the destination page:

```
await Navigation.PushAsync(new EditPage());
```

The above code pushes the new page onto the navigation stack, making it the currently active page:

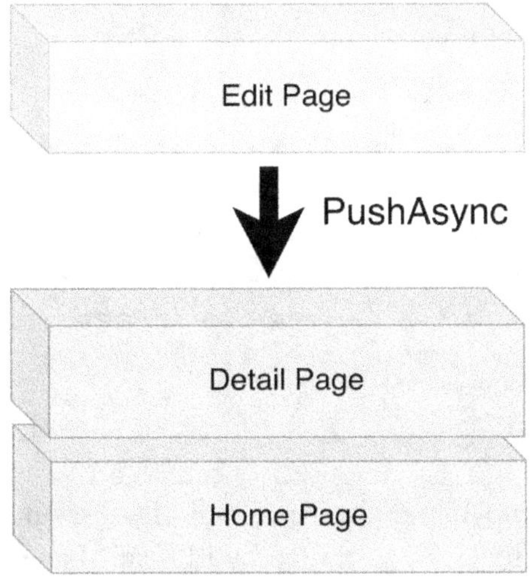


Figure 20-3

To return to the previous page, we call PopAsync() to pop the current page off the stack:

```
await Navigation.PopAsync();
```

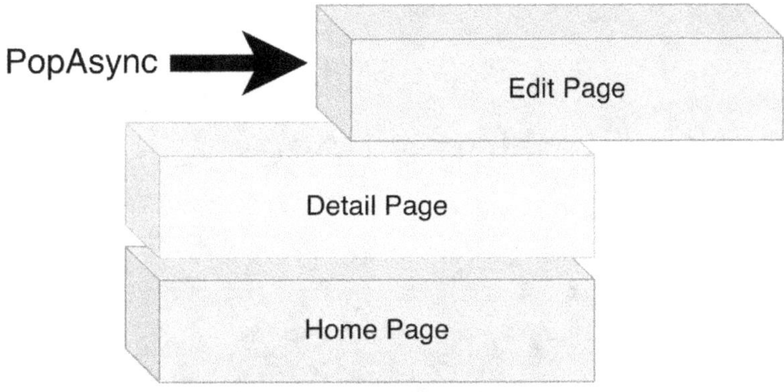


Figure 20-4

In a C# Markup application, the NavigationPage setup is typically performed in the App class declaration. With the NavDemo project loaded into Visual Studio, edit the *App.xaml.cs* file and modify it as follows:

```
namespace NavDemo
{
    public partial class App : Application
    {
        public App()
```

```
    {
        InitializeComponent();
    }


    protected override Window CreateWindow(
            ActivationState? activationState)
    {
        return new Window(new AppShell());
        return new Window(new NavigationPage(
                        new MainPage { Title = "Home" }));
    }
  }
}
```

The above change switches from using the AppShell class as the root element of our window hierarchy to a NavigationPage instance initialized with MainPage as the root page. The AppShell class is still declared in *AppShell.cs*, and we will use it again later, but for now, we are not referencing it in the app.

Build and run the app, and confirm that the home page shown in Figure 20-5 appears:

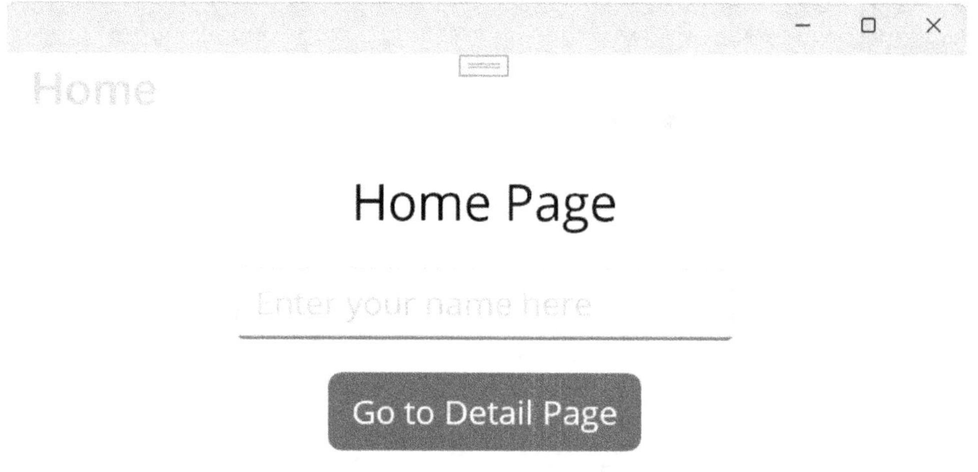


Figure 20-5

Once the application is configured in this way, any page within the navigation stack can initiate navigation via the Navigation property. To implement navigation between MainPage and DetailPage, edit *MainPage.cs* and add an event handler to the Button view that calls PushAsync():

.

.

```
public partial class MainPage : ContentPage
```

```csharp
{
    public MainPage()
    {
        Content = new VerticalStackLayout
        {
        .
        .
                        new Button()
                            .Text("Go to Detail Page")
                            .Font(size: 20)
                            .CenterHorizontal()
                            .Invoke(async btn =>
                            {
                                btn.Clicked += async (_, _) =>
                                    await btn.Navigation.PushAsync(
                                                new DetailPage());
                            })
            }
        };
    }
}
```

Next, edit the *DetailPage.cs* file and add an event handler to the topmost Button view to navigate to EditPage:

```csharp
new Button()
    .Text("Go to Edit Page")
    .Font(size: 20)
    .CenterHorizontal()
    .Invoke(async btn =>
    {
        btn.Clicked += async (_, _) =>
            await btn.Navigation.PushAsync(new EditPage());
    }),
```

Remaining in the DetailPage declaration, configure the second Button view to call PopAsync() to return to the home screen:

```csharp
new Button()
    .Text("Go Back")
    .Font(size: 20)
    .CenterHorizontal()
    .Invoke(async btn =>
    {
        btn.Clicked += async (_, _) =>
```

```
                await btn.Navigation.PopAsync();
    })
```

Edit the *EditPage.cs* file and add an event handler that calls PopAsync() to return to the detail page:

```
new Button()
    .Text("Go Back")
    .Font(size: 20)
    .CenterHorizontal()
    .Invoke(async btn =>
    {
        btn.Clicked += async (_, _) =>
            await btn.Navigation.PopAsync();
    }),
```

On the Edit page, we need the "Go Home" button to pop both the Edit page and the DetailPage entries off the stack, leaving the Home page as the current page. To do so, we can call the PopToRootAsync() method:

```
new Button()
    .Text("Go Home")
    .Font(size: 20)
    .CenterHorizontal()
    .Invoke(async btn =>
    {
        btn.Clicked += async (_, _) =>
            await btn.Navigation.PopToRootAsync();
    }),
```

With the changes complete, run the app and use the buttons to navigate between the pages. Experiment with entering text into the home page Entry and selecting a value from the detail page picker before navigating forward, then check whether the text is preserved when navigating backward. You should find that previous pages appear unchanged when navigating backward because the pages were preserved on the stack. The same is not true when navigating forwards since the original pages were popped off the stack and have to be recreated.

We now have stack-based navigation working. For a more flexible solution, we need to use the Shell's route-based navigation system.

## 20.5 A Shell-based Navigation Example

To adapt the project to Shell-based navigation, edit the *App.xaml.cs* file and restore AppShell as the root Window child:

```
  .

  .

protected override Window CreateWindow(IActivationState? activationState)
```

```
{
    return new Window(new AppShell());
    return new Window(new NavigationPage(new MainPage { Title = "Home"
}));
}
.
.
```

## 20.5.1 Adding the root navigation destination

To implement Shell-based navigation, the next step is to provide the Shell with a root navigation destination, represented by a ShellContent instance initialized with the corresponding page. This is the first page that will appear when the app launches. ShellContent instances are added by calling the Add() method of the Shell.Item property. To make MainPage the root destination, edit the *AppShell.cs* file and make the following change:

```
namespace NavDemo
{
    public partial class AppShell : Shell
    {
        public AppShell()
        {
            Items.Add(new ShellContent
            {
                Title = "Home",
                ContentTemplate = new DataTemplate(typeof(MainPage)),
                Route = "HomePage"
            });
        }
    }
}
```

Though we have added a single item, multiple items can be added to create what is known as the "Shell visual hierarchy". Note that MainPage is wrapped in a ShellContent instance. ShellContent represents the entry point to a screen within a Shell and acts as a destination marker when implementing navigation. In the above code, the ShellContent declaration assigns a route identifier to the destination ("HomePage") to which we can navigate using the Shell's GoToAsync() method, for example:

```
await Shell.Current.GoToAsync("HomePage");
```

## 20.5.2 Registering the destination route paths

With the ShellContent route defined for MainPage, the paths to the remaining pages must be registered. Remaining in the *AppShell.cs* file, register the following navigation routes:

```
namespace NavDemo
{
```

```csharp
public partial class AppShell : Shell
{
    public AppShell()
    {
        Items.Add(new ShellContent
        {
            Title = "Home",
            ContentTemplate = new DataTemplate(typeof(MainPage)),
            Route = "HomePage"
        });

        Routing.RegisterRoute("DetailPage", typeof(DetailPage));
        Routing.RegisterRoute("EditPage", typeof(EditPage));
    }
}
```

## 20.5.3 Adding the navigation method calls

As an initial navigation test, edit the *MainPage.cs* file and modify the Button view event handler to call the GoToAsync() method, passing it the route identifier for the detail screen (DetailPage) as the navigation URI:

```csharp
new Button()
    .Text("Go to Detail Page")
    .Font(size: 20)
    .CenterHorizontal()
    .Invoke(async btn =>
    {
        btn.Clicked += async (_, _) =>
            await btn.Navigation.PushAsync(new DetailPage();
            await Shell.Current.GoToAsync("DetailPage");
    })
```

Repeat the above step in the *DetailPage.cs* file, this time referencing the EditPage route identifier as the navigation URI in the topmost Button event handler:

```csharp
new Button()
    .Text("Go to Edit Page")
    .Font(size: 20)
    .CenterHorizontal()
    .Invoke(async btn =>
    {
        btn.Clicked += async (_, _) =>
            await btn.Navigation.PushAsync(new EditPage();
            await Shell.Current.GoToAsync("EditPage");
```

```
}),
```

Before adding the backward navigation calls, we first need to understand the concepts of absolute and relative navigation.

### 20.5.4 Absolute vs. relative navigation

The main strength of shell-based navigation in comparison to stack-based navigation is the ability to jump directly to specific destination pages. These jumps can be performed using relative or absolute navigation. Relative navigation is performed relative to the current location in the navigation stack. Our home screen, for example, uses relative navigation to move from the home screen to the detail screen:

```
await Shell.Current.GoToAsync("DetailPage");
```

When the GoToAsync() method is called, the Shell searches for the specified route name within the current navigation stack and among pages registered with Routing.RegisterRoute. If a match is found, it is pushed onto the existing navigation stack, making it the current page.

Relative navigation can only be used for pages registered via Routing.RegisterRoute and will not work for pages defined directly in the Shell visual hierarchy.

To navigate back one level in the current navigation stack, call GotoAsync() specifying ".." as the URI, for example:

```
await Shell.Current.GoToAsync("..");
```

This call pops the current page from the stack, making the page beneath it the current page. The same technique may be used to pop multiple pages from the stack. Route identifiers can be combined to create full navigation paths. The following code, for example, pops two pages from the navigation stack:

```
await Shell.Current.GoToAsync("../..");
```

We can also combine navigation techniques. In the following example, the Shell will pop two pages from the navigation stack before pushing the Detail page onto it:

```
await Shell.Current.GoToAsync("../../DetailPage");
```

Absolute navigation is performed by prefixing the destination route with "//", for example:

```
Shell.Current.GoToAsync("//HomePage");
```

Absolute navigation ignores the current stack and searches the entire *Shell visual hierarchy*. When a match is found, it replaces the current navigation stack, essentially resetting the root to that page. As with relative navigation, absolute navigation paths can be assembled from multiple routes:

```
await Shell.Current.GoToAsync("//HomePage/DetailPage/EditPage");
```

Absolute navigation is primarily used when working with Tabs and Flyouts and typically does not work with routes registered via Routing.RegisterRoute.

Table 20-1 outlines the key aspects of absolute and relative navigation:

| Navigation Type | Syntax | Path Type | Effect on Stack | Registration |
|---|---|---|---|---|
| Relative | "DetailPage" | Relative | Pushes onto stack | Routing.RegisterRoute |
| Backward | ".." | Relative | Pops from stack | Routing.RegisterRoute |
| Absolute | "//MainPage" | Absolute | Resets/Replaces stack | Defined in AppShell hierarchy |

Table 20-1

Complete the navigation changes by modifying the *EditPage.cs* "Go Back" button to navigate back one level, and the "Go Home" button to reset the stack and navigate directly to the home page:

```
new Button()
    .Text("Go Back")
    .Font(size: 20)
    .CenterHorizontal()
    .Invoke(async btn =>
    {
        btn.Clicked += async (_, _) =>
            await btn.Navigation.PopAsync();
            await Shell.Current.GoToAsync("..");
    }),

new Button()
    .Text("Go Home")
    .Font(size: 20)
    .CenterHorizontal()
    .Invoke(async btn =>
    {
        btn.Clicked += async (_, _) =>
            await btn.Navigation.PopToRootAsync();
            await Shell.Current.GoToAsync("//HomePage");
    }),
```

Next, update the "Go Back" button in the *DetailPage.cs* file:

```
new Button()
    .Text("Go Back")
    .Font(size: 20)
    .CenterHorizontal()
    .Invoke(async btn =>
    {
        btn.Clicked += async (_, _) =>
            await btn.Navigation.PopAsync();
```

```
        await Shell.Current.GoToAsync("..");
    })
```

Run the app and test that the navigation works as intended.

## 20.6 Navigating with Parameters

When implementing navigation, it is a common requirement to pass data from one page to another. In .NET MAUI, we achieve this by configuring the destination page to accept parameters, the values for which are passed from the originating page by appending them to the URI.

The destination page can receive parameters by implementing the IQueryAttributable interface, for example:

```
public class DetailPage : ContentPage, IQueryAttributable
{
    public void ApplyQueryAttributes(IDictionary<string, object> query)
    {
        var name = query["name"];
    }
}
```

When the page is pushed onto the stack, it is passed a Dictionary object containing key/value pairs that transfer the data. To pass a value for the id property in the above example, we reference it in the navigation URI using query string syntax as follows:

```
await Shell.Current.GoToAsync("DetailPage?id=42");
```

In the above URI, the question mark (?) marks the start of the query string, which contains named parameters passed along with the route. Everything before the question mark identifies the destination, while everything after supplies additional data in key–value pairs separated by ampersands.

We can also configure a page to receive multiple parameters, for example:

```
public class DetailPage : ContentPage, IQueryAttributable
{
    public string Id { get; private set; }
    public string Name { get; private set; }
    public string Title { get; private set; }
    public bool Favorite { get; private set; }

    public void ApplyQueryAttributes(IDictionary<string, object> query)
    {
        Id = query["id"]?.ToString();
        Name = query["name"]?.ToString();
        Title = query["title"]?.ToString();

        if (bool.TryParse(query["favorite"]?.ToString(), out var fav))
```

Navigation and Shell Integration

```
            Favorite = fav;
    }
}
```

When navigating to the page, we might use the following URI:

```
"DetailPage?id=42&name=Jane&title=Manager&favorite=true"
```

Navigation parameters may also be used to pass non-string values, including custom objects, between pages. Consider the following custom class containing contact detail properties:

```
public class Contact
{
    public string Id { get; set; }
    public string Name { get; set; }
    public string Title { get; set; }
    public bool Favorite { get; set; }
}
```

We can now create a Contact object instance and pass it directly to the DetailPage without using a query string:

```
var contact = new Contact
{
    Id = "42",
    Name = "Jane Doe",
    Title = "Senior Developer",
    Favorite = true
};

await Shell.Current.GoToAsync("DetailPage", new Dictionary<string,
object>
{
    ["contact"] = contact
});
```

To receive the object in the destination page, we could use the following IQueryAttributable declaration:

```
public class ContactDetailPage : ContentPage, IQueryAttributable
{
    public Contact? Contact { get; private set; }

    public void ApplyQueryAttributes(IDictionary<string, object> query)
    {
        if (query.TryGetValue("contact", out var value) &&
            value is Contact contact)
        {
```

```
        Contact = contact;
        var name = contact.Name;



    }

  }

}
```

The assignment "Contact = contact" copies the object from a temporary local variable into a page property. Because local variables exist only for the duration of the method call, failing to store the value would cause the object to be lost once ApplyQueryAttributes returns. Persisting it in a property allows the page to access the data later for binding, layout, and user interaction.

As the final step in the demo project, edit the Button view in *MainPage.cs* to extract the name entered into the Entry, and pass it to DetailPage:

```
new Button()
    .Text("Go to Detail Page")
    .Font(size: 20)
    .CenterHorizontal()
    .Invoke(async btn =>
    {
        btn.Clicked += async (_, _) =>
        {
            var text = inputEntry.Text ?? string.Empty;
            await Shell.Current.GoToAsync($"DetailPage?name={text}");
        };
    })
```

Finally, edit the *DetailPage.cs* file to declare the parameter and apply it to  the Label text:

```
public partial class DetailPage : ContentPage, IQueryAttributable
{
    private readonly Label _greeting;

    public DetailPage()
    {
        _greeting = new Label()
            .Font(size: 30)
            .CenterHorizontal();
```

```
        Content = new VerticalStackLayout
        {

.

.

        };
    }


    public void ApplyQueryAttributes(IDictionary<string, object> query)
    {
        if (query == null)
            return;

        if (query.TryGetValue("name", out var value)
                            && value is string name)
        {
            _greeting.Text = $"Welcome {name}";
        }
    }
}
```

Rerun the app, enter a name on the home page, and verify that it appears in the welcome message when you navigate to the detail page.

## 20.7 Summary

In this chapter, we migrated the AppShell from XAML into C# Markup and explored how navigation is implemented within a .NET MAUI application. After reviewing the internal application hierarchy and the roles played by App, Window, Page, and Shell, we saw how this structure forms the foundation for all navigation behavior.

We first implemented stack-based navigation using NavigationPage and the PushAsync() and PopAsync() methods to move forward and backward through a page stack. We then introduced Shell-based navigation, defining destinations with ShellContent, registering routes, and navigating using URI paths and the GoToAsync() method. Relative and absolute routing provided flexible control over how pages are added to or replaced on the stack.

Finally, we demonstrated how to pass both simple values and complex objects between pages using navigation parameters and the IQueryAttributable interface. With these techniques, you can build clear, maintainable navigation flows entirely in C# without relying on XAML.

# 21. Navigation with Flyouts and Tab Bars

In previous chapters, we explored how navigation can be performed in .NET MAUI by pushing and popping pages on the navigation stack and by using Shell routes to move between destinations. While these techniques work well for simple workflows, most real-world applications require a higher-level navigation structure that allows users to switch between major app areas quickly.

For example, an application might contain a dashboard, a settings screen, and a reports section. Navigating between these areas using only push navigation would quickly become cumbersome and unintuitive. Users typically expect to switch between top-level areas using either a side menu or a row of tabs.

The .NET MAUI Shell provides two built-in solutions to this problem in the form of flyouts and tab bars. A flyout presents a sliding menu containing navigation destinations, while a tab bar displays destinations along the bottom or top of the screen. Both approaches organize an application into clearly defined sections and simplify movement between them.

This chapter demonstrates how to implement both flyout and tab-based navigation using C# Markup without relying on XAML.

## 21.1 Understanding Shell Navigation Containers

Shell organizes navigation using a hierarchy of container objects. At the top level is the Shell itself, which contains one or more items representing major areas of the application.

Each item can be one of the following:

- **FlyoutItem** – Appears in the flyout menu

- **Tab** – Represents a single tab within a tab bar

- **ShellContent** – Hosts the actual page

These containers can be nested. For example, a flyout item may contain multiple tabs, with each tab displaying a different page.

Later in this chapter, we will create a project that demonstrates flyout and tab bar implementation and behavior. The hierarchy tree of the finished app is illustrated in Figure 21-1 below.

In the diagram, each branch represents a top-level destination. When the user selects an item, Shell automatically displays the associated content and maintains the correct navigation stack:

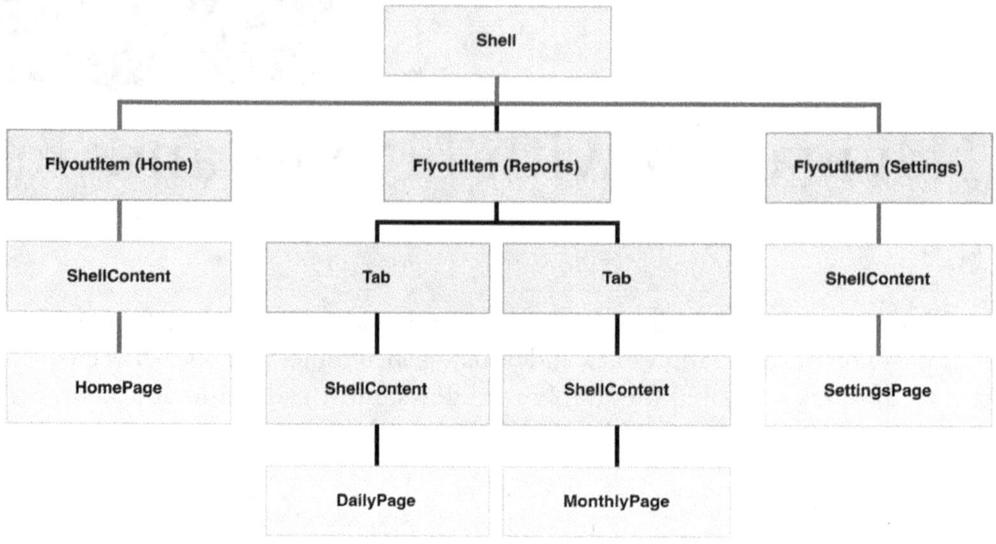

Figure 21-1

## 21.2 Why Use Flyouts and Tabs?

Flyouts and tabs solve different navigation problems, and each is suited to a particular type of application structure. A flyout works best when an application contains a large number of sections or when screen space is limited. Because the menu remains hidden until needed, it keeps the interface uncluttered while still providing access to less frequently used areas of the app. This makes the flyout particularly useful for secondary or occasionally accessed features.

A tab bar, in contrast, is more appropriate when only a small number of primary sections are required, and users regularly switch between them. By keeping these destinations visible at all times, tabs provide quick, one-tap access and make frequent navigation faster and more intuitive.

These approaches are not mutually exclusive and can also be combined. For example, a flyout item can host a set of tabs, allowing users to select major application areas from the flyout. In contrast, closely related views within those areas are accessed via tabs. Because Shell automatically manages most of the underlying behavior, implementing these navigation patterns in C# Markup primarily involves constructing the correct hierarchy of container objects rather than writing custom navigation logic.

## 21.3 Creating the FlyoutTabDemo Project

Start Visual Studio and create a new project named FlyoutTabDemo using the MauiMarkup project template.

To adapt the project to Shell-based navigation, edit the *App.xaml.cs* file and restore AppShell as the root Window child:

```
.
.
protected override Window CreateWindow(IActivationState? activationState)
{
```

```
    return new Window(new AppShell());
    return new Window(new NavigationPage(new MainPage { Title = "Home"
}));
}
.
.
```

Open *AppShell.cs* and replace the existing content with an empty Shell class:

```
public class AppShell : Shell
{
    public AppShell()
    {
    }
}
```

Next, open *App.xaml.cs* and set the main page to an instance of AppShell:

```
MainPage = new AppShell();
```

## 21.4 Designing the Destination Pages

Before adding navigation containers, we will create some simple pages that will act as navigation destinations, beginning with the home page in the *MainPage.cs* file:

```
namespace FlyoutTabDemo
{
    public partial class MainPage : ContentPage
    {
        public MainPage()
        {
            Content = new Label
            {
                Text = "Home Page",
                HorizontalOptions = LayoutOptions.Center,
                VerticalOptions = LayoutOptions.Center
            };
        }
    }
}
```

Next, open the Solution Explorer panel, right-click on the top-level FlyoutItemDemo entry, and select the *Add -> Class...* menu option to add a new class file named *DemoPages.cs*. Use this new class to declare two additional pages:

```
namespace MauiDemo
{
    public partial class DailyPage : ContentPage
    {
```

```csharp
        public DailyPage()
        {

            Title = "Daily";
            Content = new Label
            {

                Text = "Daily Report",
                HorizontalOptions = LayoutOptions.Center,
                VerticalOptions = LayoutOptions.Center
            };

        }

    }


    public partial class MonthlyPage : ContentPage
    {

        public MonthlyPage()
        {

            Title = "Monthly";

            Content = new Label
            {

                Text = "Monthly Report",
                HorizontalOptions = LayoutOptions.Center,
                VerticalOptions = LayoutOptions.Center
            };

        }

    }


    public partial class SettingsPage : ContentPage
    {

        public SettingsPage()
        {

            Title = "Settings";

            Content = new Label
            {

                Text = "Settings Page",
                HorizontalOptions = LayoutOptions.Center,
                VerticalOptions = LayoutOptions.Center
            };

        }

    }
```

```
}
```

## 21.5 Adding Flyout Navigation

The next step is to configure the Shell so that these pages appear in the flyout menu. Edit *AppShell. xaml.cs* and make the following changes:

```
public class AppShell : Shell
{
    public AppShell()
    {
        InitializeComponent();
        Items.Add(new FlyoutItem
        {
            Title = "Home",
            Route = "HomePage",
            Items =
            {
                new ShellContent
                {
                    ContentTemplate = new DataTemplate(typeof(MainPage))
                }
            }
        });

        Items.Add(new FlyoutItem
        {
            Title = "Settings",
            Route = "SettingsPage",
            Items =
            {
                new ShellContent
                {
                    ContentTemplate = new DataTemplate(
                                    typeof(SettingsPage))
                }
            }
        });
    }
}
```

The AppShell class derives from the Shell class and serves as the root navigation container for the entire application. All top-level navigation structure is defined within this class. Rather than pushing and popping pages manually, we construct a hierarchy of Shell items and let Shell handle the navigation automatically.

In the above code, destinations are added to the Shell by appending items to the Items collection. Each entry added to this collection represents a top-level section of the application that will appear in the flyout menu. In this example, two FlyoutItem instances are created.

Each FlyoutItem defines a Title property that specifies the text displayed in the flyout menu and a Route value that uniquely identifies the destination. The route allows the section to be selected programmatically using methods such as GoToAsync(). This means that navigating to "settings", for example, will automatically activate the corresponding flyout item.

A FlyoutItem does not display content directly. Instead, it hosts one or more ShellContent objects. A ShellContent instance serves as a wrapper for the page to display when the item is selected. In this case, the Home flyout item contains a ShellContent configured to display a HomePage instance, while the Settings item displays a SettingsPage.

Run the app, select the flyout menu button to display the flyout panel, and note that selecting an item from the menu automatically replaces the visible content with the associated page:

Figure 21-2

## 21.6 Adding a Tab Bar

The next step is to add the Reports navigation option to the Shell Items collection, which uses tabs to provide access to the Daily and Monthly pages. Remaining in the AppShell class declaration, make the following changes:

```
public partial class AppShell : Shell
{
    public AppShell()
    {
        Items.Add(new FlyoutItem
        {
            Title = "Home",
.
.
        });
```

```
Items.Add(new FlyoutItem
{
    Title = "Reports",
    Items =
    {
        new Tab
        {
            Title = "Daily",
            Items =
            {
                new ShellContent
                {
                    ContentTemplate =
                        new DataTemplate(typeof(DailyPage))
                }
            }
        },
        new Tab
        {
            Title = "Monthly",
            Items =
            {
                new ShellContent
                {
                    ContentTemplate =
                        new DataTemplate(typeof(MonthlyPage))
                }
            }
        }
    }
});

Items.Add(new FlyoutItem
{
    Title = "Settings",

    .

    .

});
    }
}
```

This statement adds a new FlyoutItem to the Shell that represents the application's Reports section. As with the previous examples, adding the item to the Items collection registers it as a top-level destination that will appear in the flyout menu. The Title property specifies the text displayed to the user, while the Route value uniquely identifies this section so it can be selected programmatically using a call such as GoToAsync("reports").

Unlike the earlier flyout items, this destination does not display a single page. Instead, it creates a tab bar with the two tab items, allowing multiple related pages to be grouped in the Reports section. This demonstrates how Shell containers can be nested to create more sophisticated navigation structures. Selecting Reports from the flyout activates the section, after which the tab bar provides navigation between the pages it contains.

The FlyoutDisplayOptions property is set to AsMultipleItems so that the tab structure is presented clearly within the flyout interface rather than being collapsed into a single entry. This makes each subsection easier to discover and emphasizes that Reports contains multiple views.

Inside the Reports item, two Tab instances are created with the titles "Daily" and "Monthly". Each tab represents an individual view within the Reports section. As with flyout items, a tab does not host content directly. Instead, each contains a ShellContent object that wraps the page to be displayed. The first tab displays a DailyPage, while the second displays a MonthlyPage.

When the application runs, selecting Reports reveals the tab bar containing the tabs by default. Switching tabs replaces the visible content without pushing new pages onto the navigation stack. In this way, the flyout controls movement between major sections of the app, while the tab bar enables quick switching between closely related views within a section, all without requiring any custom navigation logic.

## 21.7 Testing the Application

Run the application, open the flyout menu, and select Home or Settings. The content should update immediately. Next, select Reports. A tab bar should appear containing the Daily and Monthly tabs. Switching between the tabs should not push pages onto the navigation stack but instead replace the visible content:

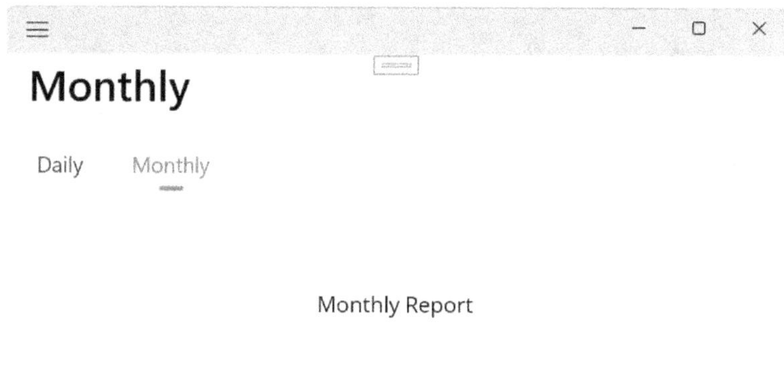


Figure 21-3

This demonstrates the key difference between hierarchical navigation and section-based navigation. Flyouts and tabs change the active section, while push navigation moves deeper within a section.

## 21.8 Summary

This chapter has introduced flyout and tab-based navigation in .NET MAUI Shell using C# Markup. Flyouts provide a convenient way to organize an application into major sections, while tab bars allow quick switching between closely related views. By constructing the appropriate hierarchy of FlyoutItem, Tab, and ShellContent objects, complex navigation structures can be created without writing any custom navigation logic.

With these containers in place, Shell automatically manages page presentation and navigation behavior, allowing you to focus on building the application's functionality rather than implementing infrastructure code.

# 22. An Introduction to Animations and Effects

User interfaces are not only about layout and functionality but also about how they respond to user interaction. Subtle animations and visual effects can make an application feel more responsive, intuitive, and polished. For example, a button that briefly scales when tapped or a view that smoothly transitions into position gives immediate feedback to the user and helps guide attention.

In .NET MAUI, animations are built directly into the framework and can be applied to any visual element. When working with C# Markup, these animations are implemented programmatically, giving you precise control over when they run, how long they take, and how different animations are combined.

This chapter explores how animations work in .NET MAUI and demonstrates how to implement them using C# Markup, beginning with simple examples and gradually building toward more advanced effects.

## 22.1 Understanding How Animations Work

At a fundamental level, an animation in .NET MAUI is a gradual change of a property value over time. For example, when a view fades out, its Opacity property is not set to 0.0 instantly. Instead, the value is updated incrementally over a specified duration, creating the appearance of a smooth transition.

Each animation method, such as FadeToAsync() or TranslateToAsync(), performs this interpolation internally. You specify a target value and a duration, and the framework calculates the intermediate values needed to move from the current state to the target state.

Animations in .NET MAUI are asynchronous operations. This means they run over time without blocking the rest of the application. Each animation method returns a Task, allowing it to be awaited. When you await an animation, execution pauses until the animation completes, making it easy to sequence multiple animations.

## 22.2 Creating the AnimationDemo Project

Launch Visual Studio and create a new .NET MAUI project named AnimationDemo using our C# Markup template.

Open the *MainPage.cs* file and make the following modifications:

```
using CommunityToolkit.Maui.Markup;
using Microsoft.Maui.Layouts;
```

```csharp
namespace AnimationDemo
{
    public partial class MainPage : ContentPage
    {
        private readonly Label _label;

        public MainPage()
        {
            _label = new Label()
                .Text("Animate Me")
                .Font(size: 36)
                .CenterHorizontal();

            Content = new FlexLayout
            {
                Direction = FlexDirection.Column,
                JustifyContent = FlexJustify.SpaceEvenly,
                AlignItems = FlexAlignItems.Center,
                VerticalOptions = LayoutOptions.Fill,

                Children =
                {
                    _label,
                    new Button()
                        .Text("Start Animation")
                        .CenterHorizontal()
                        .Invoke(btn =>
                        {
                            btn.Clicked += async (_, _) =>
                            {
                                await RunAnimation();
                            };
                        })
                }
            };
        }

        private async Task RunAnimation()
        {
```

```
        }
    }
}
```

In this layout, a Label is stored in a field so that it can be accessed later by the animation logic. The Button is configured with a Clicked event handler that calls the RunAnimation() method. Because animations are asynchronous, the event handler is declared with the async keyword and must *await* the animation method call. Build and run the app, which should appear as illustrated in Figure 22-1:

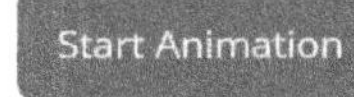


Figure 22-1

## 22.3 Implementing a Basic Fade Animation

To implement the fading animation effect, add the following code to the RunAnimation method:

```
private async Task RunAnimation()
{
    await _label.FadeToAsync(0.2, 1000);
    await _label.FadeToAsync(1.0, 1000);
}
```

The FadeToAsync() method animates the view's Opacity property. The first parameter specifies the target opacity, while the second defines the duration in milliseconds.

An Introduction to Animations and Effects

When this code runs, the label's opacity does not change instantly. Instead, .NET MAUI gradually adjusts the Opacity value over 1000 milliseconds until it reaches 0.2. Because the method is awaited, the second FadeToAsync() call does not begin until the first animation has completed. This creates a sequence where the label fades out and then fades back in.

## 22.4 Combining Animations

Animations can be executed sequentially or in parallel. Sequential animations are created using await, as seen in the previous example. To run animations simultaneously, Task.WhenAll() can be used. Modify the RunAnimation() method as follows to see this in action:

```
private async Task RunAnimation()
{
    await Task.WhenAll(
        _label.TranslateToAsync(0, 100, 500),
        _label.ScaleToAsync(1.5, 500)
    );

    await Task.WhenAll(
        _label.TranslateToAsync(0, 0, 500),
        _label.ScaleToAsync(1.0, 500)
    );
}
```

The TranslateToAsync() method animates the view's position, while ScaleToAsync() animates its size. Because both animations are included in a Task.WhenAll() call, they run at the same time.

Internally, each animation updates a different property of the view. TranslateToAsync() modifies the translation offset, while ScaleToAsync() adjusts the scale factor. Since these properties are independent, they can be animated concurrently without conflict.

## 22.5 Adding Rotation

Rotation is handled by the RotateToAsync() method in a similar way to the other animation methods:

```
private async Task RunAnimation()
{
    await _label.RotateToAsync(360, 1000);
    _label.Rotation = 0;
}
```

The RotateToAsync() method animates the Rotation property from its current value to the specified target. In this case, the label rotates through 360 degrees over one second:

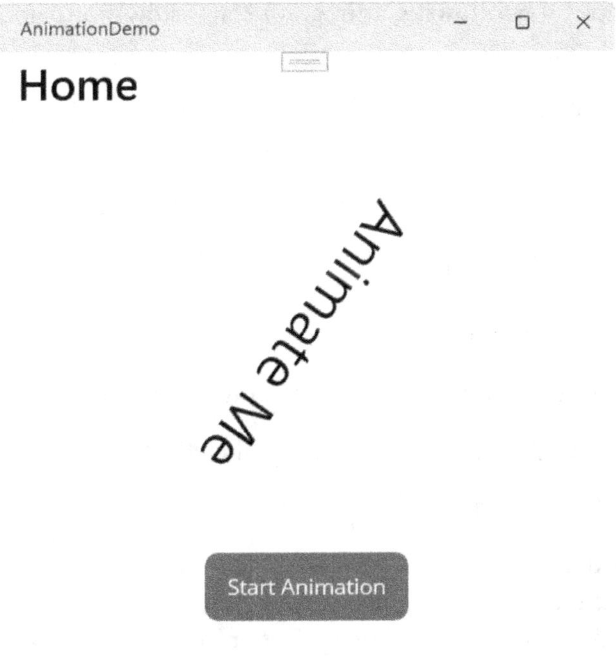


Figure 22-2

Once the animation completes, the Rotation property is manually reset to 0. This is necessary because the rotation value persists after the animation, and repeated animations would otherwise continue accumulating rotation.

## 22.6 Using Easing Functions

By default, animations progress at a constant speed from start to finish. While this linear motion is simple, it often feels unnatural. In the real world, objects tend to accelerate and decelerate rather than move at a fixed rate. Easing functions are used to simulate these more natural motion patterns.

An easing function modifies how the animation progresses over time by adjusting the rate at which intermediate values are calculated. Instead of moving evenly between the starting and ending values, the animation can start slowly, speed up, slow down, or even bounce at the end.

For example, the following animation uses a bounce effect:

```
await _label.TranslateToAsync(0, 100, 500, Easing.BounceOut);
```

In this case, the view moves toward its destination and then briefly "bounces" before coming to rest. This type of easing is often used to draw attention to an element or provide a playful visual effect.

.NET MAUI provides a range of built-in easing functions, each producing a different motion characteristic. For example, the following animation starts slowly and accelerates toward the end:

```
await _label.TranslateToAsync(0, 100, 500, Easing.CubicIn);
```

Conversely, the following begins quickly and slows down as it approaches the destination:

```
await _label.TranslateToAsyc(0, 100, 500, Easing.CubicOut);
```

To create a smooth transition that both accelerates and decelerates, the following easing function can be used:

```
await _label.TranslateToAsynv(0, 100, 500, Easing.CubicInOut);
```

Other commonly used easing functions include:

- Easing.SinIn, SinOut, and SinInOut for smooth, sinusoidal motion

- Easing.SpringIn and SpringOut for elastic, spring-like effects

- Easing.Linear for constant-speed motion

Each easing function provides a distinct visual feel, and selecting the appropriate one depends on the animation's context. Subtle easing is typically preferred for standard UI transitions, while more pronounced effects such as bounce or spring animations are useful for highlighting user interactions.

## 22.7 Responding to User Interaction

Animations are often used to provide feedback when the user interacts with the interface.

For example:

```
namespace AnimationDemo
{
    public partial class MainPage : ContentPage
    {
        private readonly Label _label;

        public MainPage()
        {
            _label = new Label()
                        .Text("Animate Me")
                        .Font(size: 36)
                        .CenterHorizontal();

            _label.GestureRecognizers.Add(
                new TapGestureRecognizer
                {
                    Command = new Command(async () =>
                    {
                        await _label.ScaleToAsync(1.2, 100);
```

```
                    await _label.ScaleToAsync(1.0, 100);
            })
        });


        Content = new FlexLayout
.

.
```

When the label is tapped, the ScaleToAsync() method temporarily increases its size, then returns it to its original size, creating a visual confirmation of the interaction.

## 22.8 Working with Visual Effects

In addition to animations, visual effects can enhance the appearance of UI elements.

For example:

```
public MainPage()
{
    _label = new Label()
                    .Text("Animate Me")
                    .Font(size: 36)
                    .CenterHorizontal();

    _label.Shadow = new Shadow
    {
        Offset = new Point(5, 5),
        Opacity = 0.5f,
        Radius = 10
    };
.

.
```

This code applies a shadow effect to the label as shown in Figure 22-3:

# Animate Me

Figure 22-3

Unlike animations, this change is applied immediately. However, the same properties can also be animated if needed. For example, you could animate the Opacity of a shadow or combine it with scaling effects to create a sense of depth.

## 22.9 Animating Layout Changes

Animations can also be applied when dynamically modifying the layout. In the example below, the label is initially invisible because its Opacity is set to 0. After being added to the layout, FadeToAsync() gradually increases its opacity, creating a smooth transition into view. This technique is particularly useful when updating lists or dynamically adding content:

```
var newLabel = new Label { Text = "New Item", Opacity = 0 };

layout.Add(newLabel);

await newLabel.FadeToAsync(1, 500);
```

## 22.10 Summary

In this chapter, we explored how animations work in .NET MAUI and how to implement them using C# Markup. We examined how animations modify view properties over time, how asynchronous execution enables sequencing and combining animations, and how easing functions influence motion. We also applied animations in response to user interaction and during layout updates. These techniques provide a foundation for creating responsive and visually engaging user interfaces.

# 23. Handling Gestures

Modern mobile applications rely heavily on touch-based interaction. Users expect to tap, swipe, drag, and pinch elements on the screen and receive immediate feedback. While standard controls such as buttons provide built-in interaction behavior, many scenarios require more flexible and customized input handling.

In .NET MAUI, this is achieved through gesture recognizers. Gesture recognizers allow you to detect user interactions, such as taps, swipes, and panning, and respond accordingly. When working with C# Markup, these recognizers are added and configured directly in code, giving you full control over how interactions are handled.

In this chapter, we will explore how gesture detection works in .NET MAUI and how to implement it using C# Markup. We will begin with simple tap gestures and gradually move on to more advanced interactions.

## 23.1 Understanding Gesture Recognizers

A gesture recognizer is an object that listens for a specific type of user interaction and triggers an action when that interaction occurs. Each recognizer is associated with a view and is added to its GestureRecognizers collection.

For example, a TapGestureRecognizer listens for tap events, while a PanGestureRecognizer detects dragging motions across the screen.

Internally, gesture recognizers monitor low-level touch input events generated by the operating system. When a sequence of touch events matches the pattern of a known gesture, the recognizer raises an event or executes a command.

## 23.2 Creating the GestureDemo Project

Launch Visual Studio and create a new .NET MAUI project named GestureDemo using your C# Markup template.

Open the *MainPage.cs* file and replace the existing content with the following layout:

```csharp
public partial class MainPage : ContentPage
{
    private readonly Label _label;


    public MainPage()
    {
        _label = new Label()
            .Text("Tap Me")
```

```
            .Font(size: 36)
            .CenterHorizontal();


    Content = new VerticalStackLayout
    {
        Spacing = 20,
        Children =
        {
            _label
        }
    };
    }
}
```

This layout contains a single Label that will respond to user gestures once recognizers have been applied.

## 23.3 Detecting Tap Gestures

The simplest gesture to implement is a tap. Add a TapGestureRecognizer to the label as outlined below:

```
public partial class MainPage : ContentPage
{
    private readonly Label _label;

    public MainPage()
    {
        _label = new Label()
        .Text("Tap Me")
        .Font(size: 36)
        .CenterHorizontal();

        _label.GestureRecognizers.Add(
            new TapGestureRecognizer
            {
                Command = new Command(() =>
                {
                    _label.Text = "Tapped!";
                })
            });
        .
        .
```

When the user taps the label, the Command is executed, and the text updated.

The TapGestureRecognizer detects a quick touch-and-release interaction within a small area. Once this pattern is recognized, the command is invoked.

## 23.4 Handling Tap Events vs Commands

Gesture recognizers can respond using either commands or events. The previous example used a Command, which integrates well with MVVM. Alternatively, you can handle the Tapped event directly:

```
public MainPage()
{
    _label = new Label()
    .Text("Tap Me")
    .Font(size: 36)
    .CenterHorizontal();

    var tapGesture = new TapGestureRecognizer();

    tapGesture.Tapped += (_, _) =>
    {
        _label.Text = "Tapped via Event!";
    };

    _label.GestureRecognizers.Add(tapGesture);
    .
    .
```

Both approaches achieve the same result. Commands are typically used when binding to view models, while events are often simpler for code-behind implementations.

## 23.5 Detecting Double Taps

A TapGestureRecognizer can also be adapted to detect multiple taps as outlined below:

```
public MainPage()
{
    _label = new Label()
    .Text("Double Tap Me")
    .Font(size: 36)
    .CenterHorizontal();

    _label.GestureRecognizers.Add(
        new TapGestureRecognizer
        {
            NumberOfTapsRequired = 2,
            Command = new Command(() =>
            {
```

```
            _label.Text = "Double Tapped!";
        })
    });
```

.
.
.

By setting NumberOfTapsRequired, the recognizer waits for multiple taps in quick succession before triggering.

## 23.6 Handling Pan Gestures

Pan gestures allow the user to drag a view across the screen and are implemented as follows:

```
public MainPage()
{
    _label = new Label()
    .Text("Drag Me")
    .Font(size: 36)
    .CenterHorizontal();

    var panGesture = new PanGestureRecognizer();

    panGesture.PanUpdated += (s, e) =>
    {
        if (e.StatusType == GestureStatus.Running)
        {
            _label.TranslationX = e.TotalX;
            _label.TranslationY = e.TotalY;
        }
    };

    _label.GestureRecognizers.Add(panGesture);
```

.
.
.

The PanUpdated event is raised continuously as the user moves their finger. The TotalX and TotalY values represent how far the finger has moved since the gesture began.

By assigning these values to TranslationX and TranslationY, the label follows the movement of the user's finger or mouse pointer.

## 23.7 Detecting Swipe Gestures

Swipe gestures detect quick directional movements:

```
public MainPage()
{
    _label = new Label()
```

```
.Text("Swipe Me")
.Font(size: 36)
.CenterHorizontal();


_label.GestureRecognizers.Add(
    new SwipeGestureRecognizer
    {
        Direction = SwipeDirection.Left,
        Command = new Command(() =>
        {
            _label.Text = "Swiped Left";
        })
    });
```

.
.

The Direction property specifies which swipe to detect. When the gesture is recognized, the associated command is executed.

## 23.8 Handling Pinch Gestures

Pinch gestures allow zooming using the following syntax:

```
public MainPage()
{
    _label = new Label()
    .Text("Pinch Me")
    .Font(size: 36)
    .CenterHorizontal();


    var pinchGesture = new PinchGestureRecognizer();


    pinchGesture.PinchUpdated += (s, e) =>
    {
        if (e.Status == GestureStatus.Running)
        {
            _label.Scale *= e.Scale;
        }
    };


    _label.GestureRecognizers.Add(pinchGesture);
```

.
.

The Scale value represents how much the user has zoomed in or out. This value is applied to the view's Scale property, dynamically resizing it.

## 23.9 Combining Gestures and Animations

Gestures are often combined with animations to provide feedback:

```csharp
public MainPage()
{
    _label = new Label()
    .Text("Tap Me")
    .Font(size: 36)
    .CenterHorizontal();

    _label.GestureRecognizers.Add(
        new TapGestureRecognizer
        {
            Command = new Command(async () =>
            {
                await _label.ScaleToAsync(1.2, 100);
                await _label.ScaleToAsync(1.0, 100);
            })
        });

    Content = new VerticalStackLayout
    {
        Spacing = 20,
        Children =
        {
            _label
        }
    };
    .
    .
```

Here, the tap gesture triggers a short scaling animation, making the interaction feel more responsive.

## 23.10 Gesture Conflicts and Best Practices

When multiple gesture recognizers are attached to the same view, conflicts can occur. For example, a tap gesture may interfere with a swipe gesture if both are listening for similar input patterns.

To avoid issues, ensure that gestures are clearly defined and appropriate for the intended interaction. In some cases, separating gestures across different views may provide a better user experience.

Providing visual feedback, such as animations, also helps users understand when their input has been successfully recognized.

## 23.11 Summary

In this chapter, we explored how to detect and handle user gestures in a .NET MAUI application using C# Markup. We implemented tap, double-tap, pan, swipe, and pinch gestures, and examined how gesture recognizers interpret touch input and trigger actions. We also combined gestures with animations to enhance user interaction. These techniques provide a flexible foundation for building responsive, touch-driven user interfaces.

# Index

## Symbols

# Index

# Index

9 781965 764411